JEFF KINLEY

GOD'S GRAND FINALE

HARVEST PROPHECY
AN IMPRINT OF HARVEST HOUSE PUBLISHERS

Cover design by Brock Book Design Co., Charles Brock

Cover photo © tomertu, KE. Take a photo / Adobe Stock

Interior design by Aesthetic Soup

Published in association with William K. Jensen Literary Agency, 119 Bampton Court, Eugene, Oregon 97404.

For bulk, special sales, or ministry purchases, please call 1-800-547-8979.
Email: Customerservice@hhpbooks.com

God's Grand Finale
Copyright © 2023 by Jeff Kinley
Published by Harvest House Publishers
Eugene, Oregon 97408
www.harvesthousepublishers.com

ISBN 978-0-7369-8647-2 (pbk)
ISBN 978-0-7369-8648-9 (eBook)

Library of Congress Control Number: 2022945922

Printed in the United States of America

23 24 25 26 27 28 29 30 31 / BP / 10 9 8 7 6 5 4 3 2

CONTENTS

SEEING GOD IN THE STORY OF EARTH'S FINAL DAYS

Revelation tells the story of Earth's final days. It chronicles the culmination of human history. The climax of civilization. The end of all things as we know it. In the Bible's last book, we are carried to an apocalyptic intersection where crisis, chaos, and calamity all meet in a global head-on collision. It is a tale of depravity, devils, and destruction. It is the future foretold, and history written far ahead of its fulfillment.

But beyond all its prophecies and the unveiling of foretold events, Revelation is, more than anything, a book about *God*. He is the main character amid a cast that includes world leaders, miracle-working missionaries, martyrs, false prophets, apocalyptic horsemen, demonic armies and holy angels, the antichrist, the false prophet, and even the devil himself. From the pages of Scripture's closing words, it is Jesus Christ who emerges to take center stage. He is the book's central theme and its principal character. Its preeminent figure. And this is a primary reason Revelation was revealed and written. The angel who delivered this vision was right when he declared, "The testimony of Jesus *is* the spirit of prophecy" (Revelation 19:10). If you study Revelation and miss this central theme, you will walk away knowing the future but failing to know the very God who fulfills the prophecies contained within.

Inherent in its very name, Revelation appropriately begins with the revealing of Jesus Christ himself, and continues doing the same through his evaluation of the churches (chapters 2–3), the heaven where he is worshipped (chapters 4–5), the judgments he will unleash upon the planet (chapters 6–18), the climactic return he will execute from heaven (chapter 19), the kingdom over which he will reign for 1,000 years (chapter 20), and the eternal city he himself has been preparing since he left Earth 2,000 years ago (chapters 21–22).

And without a doubt, when the dust of Revelation finally settles, what you will behold is the Lamb, standing in triumph, reigning in sovereignty, and dwelling in unspeakable glory.

A.W. Tozer wrote, "The most important thing about you is what comes to your mind when you think of God."[1]

This book will cause you to think much about God. As we hike through Revelation together, you will naturally find yourself caught up in the universe of his divine attributes. The constellation of his character will surround you, challenging your thoughts while simultaneously drawing your heart into a deeper and more intimate relationship with him.

And if that is your goal, turn the page and dive in.

Jeff Kinley

CHAPTER 1

WHAT'S IN A NAME?

The God Who *Reveals*

Revelation 1:1-11

Beyond anything else, the Bible is a book about God. It's his written way of revealing himself to mankind. From Genesis to Revelation, our amazing creator has both progressively and systematically unveiled who he is, how he relates to his creation, what he has done to restore fallen humanity to himself, and what he is going to do in the future.

However, being a gracious and creative God, he chose not to limit himself to just one or two ways of communication. Rather, he has used a multitude of methods to explain himself to us.

In the Beginning, There Was...*Revelation*

God began teaching us about himself with the very first recorded words in Scripture: "In the beginning God created the heavens and the earth" (Genesis 1:1).

Written to human beings who could easily observe both the vastness of the night sky as well as the wonders and grandeur of the newly made earth, those ten words unleash a wealth of knowledge concerning God and his character. From merely observing creation, we are able to understand and deduce the following:

- God is eternal, and thus logically predates his creation. It was he who brought everything into existence out of nothing (John 1:13; Colossians 1:16; Hebrews 1:1; 11:3).
- He is supernaturally powerful, or "omnipotent" (Romans 1:20).
- He is divine and not human (Romans 1:20).
- He is creative, a master artist and architect (Psalms 8:1-4; 19).
- He is an awe-inspiring God (Job 36:32; 37:23; 38:1–39:14).
- He is a God of detail, order, and precision (see, for example, Jeremiah 33:25, where "fixed patterns" speaks of the laws of nature, physics, and physiology).

In 1820, English philosopher Herbert Spencer (himself an evolutionist) recognized five scientific principles by which he claimed we can understand the universe. They are

time
force
energy
space
matter

And yet, amazingly (and unbeknownst to Spencer), these are all specifically revealed in the very first verse of the Bible! Three thousand years before Spencer, Moses (the six-day creation guy) accurately catalogued these same complex scientific principles:

In the *beginning* [time]
God [force]

created [energy]
the *heavens* [space] and
the *earth* [matter] (Genesis 1:1).

#mindblown

So, on the very first page of the Bible, God explains in great detail and clarity what modern science still struggles to articulate. As it turns out, God is not only supreme over science, but he also invented its laws. A being possessing that level of intelligence would also lead us to conclude that he is a personal being, and not a *force*. Therefore, creation—the universe, earth, and humanity—cannot be attributed to some random chemical explosion that supposedly occurred some 14 billion years ago.

In other words, he is a big God, not a big BANG!

And all that from the first ten words of Scripture.

That's revelation.

The Evidence Speaks

We can further understand God's witness of himself to us by separating it into three categories: The first is what theologians call *general* revelation. Primarily, this refers to how the creator proclaims himself through what he has made—the universe, the earth, humankind. Creation declares both the essence of God as well as the exhibit of his handiwork (Psalm 19:1-6; Romans 1:18-20). This is his *external* witness to us. After creating the heavens and the earth using no pre-existing materials, he then prominently displayed his divine nature and glory through them so that when we look up into the night sky, we are naturally compelled to give God the glory he deserves.

Along with this external evidence, he has given us an *internal* witness as well, in two ways: First, he created us, male and female, and in his own image (Genesis 1:26-27; 2:7, 18-25). Being created in God's image means not only that we have intellect, emotion, and will, as he does, but also that we are inherently moral beings with a capacity for relationship. He made us this way so that we could worship, obey, and enjoy him.

And second, he also communicated something of himself through gifting us with a conscience (Romans 2:14-15). This is why every known secular culture throughout history has recognized and valued a basic moral code—honesty, justice, prohibitions against theft, murder, etc. The reason for this is that embedded within the human heart (mind and conscience) is an instinctive sense of right and wrong. Simply put, we feel good when we do what is right and feel guilty when we do what is wrong. Like a computer and its basic operating system, we were designed with a preinstalled conscience that is programmed to morally guide us and to reflect the knowledge of our creator and his character.

Of course, like a computer system, we can also download harmful viruses that corrupt that conscience in our human hard drive. Unfortunately, this occurred early on when Adam disobeyed God and sin infected the human race (Genesis 3:1-8). But we can also further corrupt and damage our consciences by repeatedly hardening our hearts to God's truth and revelation of himself to us (Romans 1:21). This explains why some people have lost their sensitivity to sin and to the distinction between right and wrong. Their consciences have been damaged, some irreparably so (Romans 1:28-32; Ephesians 4:17-19; 1 Timothy 4:2).

The creator made us for something more than this earth and this life. We were made for eternity (Ecclesiastes 3:11). We were made for *him* (Colossians 1:16). Even so, general revelation alone cannot lead us all the way to salvation. For that, we need God to take it to the next level.

Enter the second category—*special* revelation. Here, God graciously gives us more specific details regarding who he is and what he wants us to know about truth and life. Here are among the ways he has previously done this:

- Direct, audible communication (Genesis 2:16-17; 3:9, 11; Deuteronomy 5:4; Matthew 3:17)
- Signs and wonders (Genesis 11:1, 5-9; Exodus 14:21-31; Deuteronomy 34:10-12; 1 Kings 17–19; Psalm 78:53; 111:2-4)
- Dreams and visions (Genesis 20:6; 31:24; Job 33:14-15; Isaiah 6:1-4; Daniel 9:20-21; Matthew 1:20; 2:12-13; Revelation 1:10-16)
- Angels (Daniel 9:21; 10:13; Luke 1:11-19; Acts 7:53; Hebrews 2:2; Revelation 1:1)
- Prophets (Hebrews 1:1-3)
- Physical appearances of himself in human form in the Old Testament (Genesis 18:1-33; 32:25-28; Exodus 3:1-22; 33:18-23; Daniel 3:25), which are called *theophanies* or *Christophanies*
- Divine acts of providence (Acts 1:15-17; 17:24-28)

However, God's ultimate act of special revelation was when the second member of the Godhead became a man. This is sometimes referred to as the "incarnation of Christ" (John 1:14, 18; 12:45; 14:5; Colossians 1:15; 2:9; 1 Timothy 1:10; Titus 2:11; 3:4; Hebrews 1:1-4). The writer of Hebrews puts it this way:

> God, after He spoke long ago to the fathers in the prophets in many portions and in many ways, in these last days *has spoken to us in His Son*, whom He appointed heir of all things, through whom also He made the world. And He is the *radiance of His glory* and the *exact representation of His nature*, and upholds all things by the word of His power. When He had made purification of sins, He sat down at the right hand of the Majesty on high, having become as much better than the angels, as He has inherited a more excellent name than they (1:1-4).

The apostle John wrote,

> The Word became flesh, and dwelt among us, and we saw
> His glory, glory as of the only begotten from the Father,
> full of grace and truth…No one has seen God at any time;
> the only begotten God who is in the bosom of the Father,
> He has explained Him (John 1:14, 18).

Thankfully, the Lord also permanently documented his revelation to us in all 66 books of the Bible (2 Timothy 3:16-17). The inspired revelation of Scripture is superior to general revelation because of its specific and eternal nature (Psalm 19:9; Isaiah 40:8; Matthew 5:17-18; 24:35).

In doing this for us, God translated transcendent truth, putting it into a visual, verbal, experiential, discernable, and transferable language that virtually anyone could understand. Within Scripture's pages are realities concerning him that are easily grasped by children, coupled with concepts that even the most learned scholars struggle to comprehend.

A third way God has revealed himself is through *progressive* revelation. In other words, God (wisely) chose not to reveal all of his character, commands, or truth to any one person or all at one time. Obviously, that would have amounted to a massive information overload, and no human could have handled or processed such an experience. Instead, he gave his revelation to us in installments, or *bite-sized chunks,* if you will. Gradually, he unveiled himself and his truth over much time—through Adam, Enoch, Noah, Moses, the prophets, Jesus, and the apostles. Each new revelation built on the previous one, and the resulting portrait was one painted with both broad brushstrokes of truth as well as intricate details uncovering the beauty and wonder of our God and his magnificent plan of salvation.

And he did all this because he wanted us to know him.

So when we come to the last book of the Bible, we would expect a dramatic and powerful conclusion to God's grand story and message to us. Think about this: God could have ended his written revelation to us any way he wanted to. As an author, I do the same. I carefully consider how I conclude my books. What do I want the reader to know, think, feel, or do upon turning the last page? What do I want to impress upon him? What do I want him to remember? How do I wish him to respond? To be motivated? Inspired? Moved?

And God, being the master storyteller and consummate communicator, did the same with his book. He could have finished the Bible with a message on how to love one another, or how to be good Samaritans to our neighbors, or even by reviewing and summarizing some of the important truths he had previously communicated.

But he didn't.

Instead, he finished his magnus opus with a book that is 95 percent *prophecy*. As such, Revelation is almost exclusively a book about the future. But why? Why tell his first-century audience about prophecies that not only wouldn't end up happening in their lifetime, but wouldn't be fulfilled for at least 1,900 years?

I suppose the original hearers and readers of Genesis, Isaiah, Jeremiah, and Micah could ask the same question, for they, too, were given prophecies that were eventually fulfilled many hundreds of years after they were first given. But this highlights the very nature of prophecy—that it is primarily a foretelling of future events and not necessarily things that are happening "in the now." Some prophecies do have a near and far fulfillment to them, meaning they have significance both during the time of their revealing as well as for the time of their fulfillment (see Genesis 3:16 and John 12:31; Numbers 21:9 and John 3:14-15; Daniel 11:31 and Matthew 24:15-16; Joel 2:28-32 and Acts 2:17-21; Romans 16:20; 2 Thessalonians 2:4; Hebrews 2:14; Revelation 6:12).

So why did God end his written Word with a book on future prophetic events? Because he has unfinished business to attend to. And because...

He has a bride to rescue (John 14:1-3; 1 Thessalonians 4:13-18)

He has a people to redeem (3 Peter 3:9; Revelation 7:9-17)

He has a planet to punish (Revelation 6–19)

He has a nation to restore—Israel (Romans 11:25-26)

You see, the story isn't over. There is yet coming a climactic season-ending episode. A closing act.

A grand finale.

Fear, Fake News, and Faith

God wrote Revelation because he wants us to know about that finale, and to respond to it (Revelation 1:3). He wants us to be aware of coming world events and to spot the signs leading up to the end times. He wants us to enjoy a sneak preview of our future home in heaven. He also knew that in these last days, there would be a pandemic of confusion, ignorance, and uncertainty. Fear is currently outpacing faith among God's people. In the church, confusion is clouding clarity. Ignorance is spreading faster than knowledge. And uncertainty is overshadowing confidence.

And yet, not once in Scripture are we ever told to fear the future. Quite the opposite, as repeatedly, God instructed his people to move forward into tomorrow with faith and courage (Joshua 1:6-9; Matthew 24:3-4; 6:25-34; 1 Thessalonians 4:13; 2 Thessalonians 2:1-3; 2 Timothy 1:7). God intended for his Word to guard us against confusion, and to provide knowledge and clarity. When Paul wrote to the Thessalonians, they had become a church plagued by unsettling news from men posing as reliable teachers. Essentially, these teachers had convinced the Thessalonian believers that they had in their possession a letter from Paul indicating the day of the Lord had arrived. In other words, they claimed the rapture had already occurred and that the seven-year tribulation had begun. This information triggered at least two unpleasant concerns for the Thessalonian believers: (1) God's judgments were about to fall on the earth (and on them), and (2) they had missed their blessed hope (the rapture).

These counterfeit messengers buttressed their argument by stating they had also received a vision as well, confirming their apocalyptic assertions. The apostle wrote,

> Now we request you, brethren, with regard to the coming of our Lord Jesus Christ and our gathering together to Him, that you not be quickly shaken from your composure or be disturbed either by a spirit or a message or a letter as if from us, to the effect that the day of the Lord has come (2 Thessalonians 2:1-2).

Paul's grave concern was that this first-century fake news would shake the Thessalonians' composure and disturb their faith, which it did. So what did the apostle do? How did he respond to this troubling report? Under the Holy Spirit's divine direction, he wrote them a letter from an *actual* apostle, not a pretend one. In it, he imparted to them unquestionable and precise truth. "Let no one in any way deceive you, for it [the day of the Lord] will not come unless the apostasy comes first, and the man of lawlessness is revealed" (verse 3).

Paul wisely set the record straight. He didn't say, "Well, you know we all have our own views regarding the end times and the timing of the last-days events. But as long as we are united in the essentials of the faith, that's all that really matters. Now, all of you should just get along and love each other."

No. Unity was not Paul's chief objective here—truth was. The unity he desired for them (and for us) was to be centered on God's Word, not heretical hearsay nor rumor. He then said, "Do you not remember that while I was with you, I was telling you these things?"

(verse 5). The verb tense here indicates he had told them about these prophecies concerning the last days more than a few times. This tells us that part of Paul's core church-planting curriculum involved clear teaching about eschatology (the study of the end times). He wanted these believers to be informed on this important issue—one that today is often ignored, misunderstood, misrepresented, and miscommunicated to Christians.

Scripture always uses knowledge and understanding to combat ignorance concerning the last days—both of which are abundantly found in Bible prophecy. Often, when emphasizing the importance of studying and learning the Bible, someone will immediately counter with "We have to be careful not to learn too much, because as Paul warned, 'knowledge makes arrogant, but love edifies'" (1 Corinthians 8:1). These well-intentioned believers unknowingly undercut their own faith and spiritual growth with such statements, swinging the pendulum toward an anti-intellectual version of Christianity where our only virtue is "love." What they miss is the fact that God's truth actually transforms us by "the renewing of [our] mind" (Romans 12:2). We don't show love to people by ignoring or minimizing the truth. We love them by *telling them* the truth. Obviously, Paul was not teaching that we shouldn't pursue knowledge of Scripture. There are far too many commands and examples of such a godly pursuit elsewhere (Deuteronomy 11:18-23; Joshua 1:8; Psalm 119:11-12, 15, 23-24, 26, 33, 40, 52, 71, 93, 97-99, 100, 113, 124, 135, 152, 160, 171; Proverbs 3:1-2; 4:6-7; John 5:39; Romans 15:4; 2 Timothy 3:15, 16-17; 1 Peter 2:2; 2 Peter 3:16; Revelation 1:3).

Instead, Paul's point in 1 Corinthians 8:1 is that knowledge alone, devoid from love, only inflates one's ego. But nowhere is ignorance of Scripture exalted as a virtue to be sought after. God gives us his truth that we might know it, believe it, be convinced of it, be transformed by it, meditate on it, live by it, see the world through it, and communicate it to others.

An old adage states, "In the land of the blind, the one-eyed man is king." Similarly, in an age where ignorance, deception, and lies dominate the spiritual landscape, God's truth shines as a beacon of light in a dark night. Paul reminds us that it is the ignorance of truth, along with worldly thinking, that poses a real danger to our spirituality (1 Timothy 6:3-5). And the person who rejects the truth of God is "conceited and understands nothing" (verse 4). But not so for the biblically informed believer, as David declares:

> I have more insight than all my teachers, for your testimonies are my meditation. I understand more than the aged, because I have observed your precepts (Psalm 119:99-10).

So, the ultimate antidote to ignorance is truth—God's truth.

This revelatory knowledge given to us by God also drives out uncertainty and doubt, replacing it with genuine confidence. The prevailing spirit of our day seeks to suppress confident knowledge, especially as it relates to objective truth. Today, for a Christian to assert that God's Word is inerrant and infallible (2 Timothy 3:16-17), or that Jesus is the only way to heaven (John 14:6), is viewed as narrow and arrogant.

Narrow? Yes. But arrogant? No.

This is ironic, for we all expect this same kind of narrowmindedness in so many other areas of life. For example:

- We want our surgeon to be precise and not flippant or vague.
- We want our pharmacist to be accurate and not unsure.
- We want our pilot to be confident and not nervous.
- We want our electrician to be certain and exact, not ignorant, undecided, or sketchy.

This is even more critically important when it comes to theology, truth, morality, and reality. It is here where we need *precision*. And that's exactly what Scripture provides for us. The knowledge and clarity found in God's revelation infuses us with the very confidence we need to face our world and to forge ahead by faith.

Yes, God wants us to *know*.

Consistent with that desire, the book of Revelation is a climactic book of knowledge, not confusion. It is not an enigmatic, apocalyptic code only to be broken by a select few experts, but rather, a book of enlightenment to be read, heard, understood, and obeyed by everyone who traverses its pages (Revelation 1:3).

Like Genesis, in its very first verse, we discover Revelation to also be a book about God. It is "the Revelation of [from, about] Jesus Christ." It comes *through* an angel, *to* John, and *for* his bond-servants (the church). And what will the book also cover? "The things which must soon take place" (1:1). Revelation is the only book in the Bible that comes with a certain kind of promised *blessing* for a certain group of believers—namely, those who "read, hear, and heed the words of the prophecy" (verse 3). And why is this so important? Verse 3 concludes, "For the time is near."

CHAPTER 2

THE UNFAMILIAR JESUS

The God Who Is *Glorious*

Revelation 1:12-18

As global culture continues its descent into darkness, the shadow of a post-Christian worldview is cast on the church as well. With an ongoing departure from Scripture in favor of personal feelings, an entire subculture of emotion-based Christianity has crept into the church. This is evidenced by the often-repeated phrase, "I don't do theology. I just love Jesus."

At first glance, such a stance may sound admirable, even spiritual. For what could possibly be better, or more godly and spiritual, than to love Jesus? After all, isn't that the greatest commandment? Didn't Christ himself declare it as such in Matthew 22:36-38?

Yes.

However, as we will see, with such declarations, the church is plunged into a new dark age where ignorance and emotions become the guiding principles for the current generation of professing Christians.

And here's why: Unknowingly hidden within such a statement is an ironic contradiction. For in order to declare affection for Jesus Christ, one must have at least a minimal knowledge of who he is. Any belief in him must be based upon that revealed knowledge. It is logically impossible to love a God about whom you have no factual knowledge. And that knowledge concerning who he is, what he has done, and how he is known and loved, is called—you guessed it—*theology.*

In other words, you cannot actually love Jesus unless you "do theology." Without clear revelation about Christ, how can you ever be sure that the Jesus you love is the real one? Apart from our thoughts being informed and transformed by God's Word concerning himself (Proverbs 3:5-6; Romans 12:2), we end up with a custom-built version of Christ, one manufactured and conjured up by our own imagination.

That kind of "Jesus" is nothing more than a divine action figure, one you dress up and accessorize to fit your personal preconceptions and emotional preferences. A "do-it-yourself Jesus," if you will.

And that, tragically, is textbook idolatry.

Of course, there was and is only one real Jesus. And the only authoritative, definitive source of truth about him is found in the Bible. Apart from Scripture, we have no divinely reliable knowledge of the Son of God.

From this we can conclude that our understanding, experience, and love for Jesus is derived not from our own flawed thinking or fluctuating feelings, but rather from the totality of Scripture. As we saw in the previous chapter, in order to understand anything about God and to know him personally, he must first reveal himself to us. And we are utterly dependent on the nature, degree, and process of his revelation. Nowhere are we given permission to conjure up our own images, representations, or human interpretations of his likeness or character. Again, this is gross idolatry.

Just ask those Israelites at the foot of Mount Sinai.[1] Thankfully,

God has taken all the guesswork out of who Jesus is, and perhaps nowhere has he made it more plain and evident than in Revelation 1.

A Timely Vision

The aged apostle John has no clue what Jesus is about to reveal to him concerning the condition of the seven churches (chapters 2–3) or the catastrophic judgments of the prophesied seven-year tribulation period (chapters 6–19). But before dropping those truth bombs on him, Jesus graciously begins his final book by first revealing *himself* to the beloved disciple. But why begin Revelation this way? What's the point? Bear in mind that by AD 95, Christianity was in its third generation. The faith had been passed on for some 60 years. And some priorities needed to be reordered. I see five reasons the Bible's last book begins with a special revelation of Jesus Christ:

- to demystify errant, inaccurate human views that churches might have concerning him, both then and now.

- to refresh their memories of the Jesus who was once proclaimed to them. As we will see, several of the churches had flawed theology. They had also either forgotten Jesus or forsaken their love for him.

- to update their understanding and vision of him, as he was now glorified and exalted in heaven, seated at the right hand of the Father (Hebrews 1:3).

- to arrest their attention, dilate their spiritual eyes, and fully wake them from their complacent slumber.

- to help them worship the *true* Christ. This is how Revelation begins—with a reboot of our perception of Jesus Christ. Every truth in Revelation rests on the person and work of Jesus Christ (Revelation 19:10).

Do we not need these same things? Today's church suffers from a type of spiritual amnesia concerning her Lord, for at least four reasons:

1. We have *short* memories. Due to a current pandemic of biblical illiteracy, the church has forgotten what Jesus is like and what he has prophesied concerning the last days and God's end-times narrative.

2. We have *selective* memories. We tend to focus primarily on those attributes of Christ that give us comfort and peace (i.e., Jesus the healer, feeding the 5,000, teaching parables, suffering for us, the humble servant, the one who weeps at a funeral).

3. We tend to slumber, becoming self-obsessed and soaked in culture. We drift, sliding away from a passionate pursuit of our Savior (Revelation 2:4; 3:2).

4. We easily become complacent, mediocre, satisfied, lukewarm. This makes us ineffective for the kingdom and useless in making disciples (Matthew 28:18-20; Revelation 3:14-17).

Sound familiar? In these ways, we are not that different from our first-century brothers and sisters.

By AD 95, the church had wandered, lost her way, and in some cases, no longer resembled herself anymore. Like many churches today, she desperately needed a wake-up call.

And so, in addition to giving us front-row seats to the future and a verbal, pictorial panorama of the end times and eternity, Revelation was written to arouse a slumbering bride so she could prepare for the imminent return of the Bridegroom.

Again, because "the time is near" (Revelation 1:3).

"We wish to see Jesus"—John 12:21

So what *does* Jesus want us to know and remember about him? How are we to see and perceive him?

John's written letters to the seven churches are messages he received from Christ through his angel (Revelation 1:1). In them, he relays both grace and peace to them from the triune God—the Father (the eternal one), the seven spirits who are before the throne (representative of the Holy Spirit), and Jesus Christ (verses 4-5).[2]

Jesus in Revelation

It is here in Revelation that John is given a vision of the second member of the Godhead, Jesus Christ. And as we will discover in our journey through the book, *he* is the main character and central theme throughout. Later, in Revelation 19:10, an angel proclaims, "The testimony of Jesus is the spirit of prophecy."

So who is this "Revelation Jesus"?

Ready to do some theology?

Jesus Is Reliable (1:5)—He is called "the faithful witness." Revelation does contain some prophecies that are difficult to understand or believe, so John is assured from the beginning that the one who is revealing them is trustworthy and true. Christ himself declared to his disciples, "I am the way, the *truth*, and the life; no one comes to the Father but through Me" (John 14:6).

Jesus is not only the embodiment of truth, but truth is also at the core of his character. Consequently, he can *only* reveal the truth, because as God, it is impossible for him to lie (Numbers 23:19; Titus 1:2; Hebrews 6:18).

Here in Revelation, Jesus will bear witness to the prophetic truths concerning the state of the churches (chapters 2–3), the apocalyptic judgments of the seven-year tribulation (chapters 6–19), the millennial kingdom (chapter 20), and the eternal state (chapters 21–22). Christ was well aware that "in the last days mockers will come with

their mocking...saying, 'Where is the promise of his coming?'"
(2 Peter 3:3-4). Therefore, he begins by describing himself as the
one whose prophecies concerning future events can be trusted. The
Lord didn't give John a riddle to be solved, but a revelation to be believed. It's not a metaphoric tale laced with undecipherable symbols,
but rather, a literal scene-by-scene depiction of history, to be written down in advance of its fulfillment.

In other words, everything we read in Revelation is true because
it comes directly from the God of truth. Just as Jesus was faithful
to make known the Father's name and word to his disciples (John
17:6-8), so here now he makes known to John, and to us, the divine
prophetic truths of Revelation.

Jesus Is Risen (Revelation 1:5)—John calls Jesus "the firstborn of the
dead." The word here translated "firstborn" is *prototokos*, and speaks
of Christ's resurrection being the first of its kind (cf. Colossians 1:15).
Prior to the empty tomb, no one had ever returned from the dead
with the kind of body Jesus possessed. Scripture records miraculous
accounts of people being raised from the dead, but none compared
to Christ's resurrection.[3]

All those people would die again, unlike Jesus, who will never taste
death a second time. The good news for believers is that because he
overcame the grave, we too will be resurrected to eternal life (John
11:25; 14:19; 1 Corinthians 15:20). A dead Savior cannot impart prophecies regarding the last days. Only a living Lord can do that!

Jesus Is Ruler (Revelation 1:5)—Christ is the "ruler of the kings of
the earth." John would later record that he is also the "King of kings
and the Lord of lords" (19:16). This means that he outranks them all.
He towers over them, and possesses the authority to overrule them. It
means that his plans trump theirs. Kings, rulers, pharaohs, emperors,
caesars, prime ministers, premieres, presidents, and popes are all under
the sovereign authority of this Christ. Isaiah wrote that all the nations
are "as nothing...less than nothing" when compared to God (Isaiah

40:17). It is he who "reduces rulers to nothing, who makes the judges of the earth meaningless" (verse 23). Isaiah goes on to say,

> Scarcely have they been planted,
> scarcely have they been sown,
> scarcely has their stock taken root in the earth,
> but He merely blows on them, and they wither,
> and the storm carries them away like stubble.
> "To whom then will you liken Me
> that I would be *his* equal?" says the Holy One
> (verses 24-25).

King Nebuchadnezzar learned this lesson the hard way, being driven insane by the Lord because of his defiance and self-fueled arrogance. You can read about his experience in Daniel 4:19-37. However, upon his eventual repentance, his reason returned to him, prompting him to declare God as the ultimate sovereign (Daniel 4:34-37).

Later in Revelation, Jesus once again exercises that sovereign authority and dominion, overpowering the mightiest ruler the world has ever seen, and casting both him and his sidekick into the lake of fire after the battle of Armageddon (Revelation 19:20).

This is John's prelude to the character and person of Jesus. And he is just getting warmed up. We will get an even more specific description of him later in the same chapter.

Jesus Is Redeeming (Revelation 1:5-6)—The apostle quickly pivots here in his portrait of Christ to remind us what he has done for you and me—namely, three truths that encapsulate our relationship with him. And he does this chronologically.

1. He loves us (verse 5). And when did this love begin? According to Paul, God set his heart of love toward us in eternity past, as "He chose us in Him before the foundation of the world" (Ephesians 1:4). Lest we mistakenly believe

we had anything to do with God's motivation for loving us, Paul makes sure we understand that we weren't even around when God chose to love us. We could even argue that God, being beyond the boundaries of time, has always loved us, meaning there has never been a point in eternity past when he did not love you and me. And like his love for his covenant nation Israel, that love does not have an ending point. As Jeremiah records, "I have loved you with an everlasting love; therefore I have drawn you with lovingkindness" (Jeremiah 31:3). In Revelation 1:5, John uses the present tense, "loves," rehearsing for us the ever-present, unconditional, relevant love of Jesus. And just like his love for Israel, it leads him to act on our behalf.

2. He "released us from our sins by his blood" (verse 5). The word "released" means "to set free." At the moment of salvation, sin's grip on us was released and we were set free from the penalty of sin (Romans 5:1; 6:23; 8:1; 1 Peter 1:18-19). Therefore, there isn't an ounce of wrath or anger left toward those bought with his blood (1 Corinthians 6:20). And it's all because the Father unleashed the full fury of his righteous anger toward sin upon the Son while he hung on the cross (Matthew 27:46; Mark 15:34; 2 Corinthians 5:21). That means there is no hell for us.

However, salvation doesn't end there. Because sin's curse and *penalty* has been lifted, our identification with Jesus enables us to be saved from the *power* of sin in this current life (Romans 6:1-14). And the good news of salvation keeps getting better from there, as we are also guaranteed salvation from the *presence* of sin upon our entrance into heaven (Romans 8:29; Revelation 21:1-5). It is this very truth regarding the totality of our salvation that prompted Paul

to proclaim that nothing can ever separate us from his love
(Romans 8:31-39).

The love of God chose us, saved us, and keeps us throughout
our earthly journey, all the way to heaven, where we will
experience that love on a level not possible in this present
life.

3. He has made us to be a kingdom of priests to his God
   and Father (verse 6). As we will see in Revelation 20, we
   are guaranteed a special place in God's future kingdom.
   And by virtue of Christ's substitutionary sacrifice, we
   all become "priests to His God," meaning we have
   unrestricted access to God's presence. There, we find
   perpetual mercy at his throne of grace (Hebrews 4:14-16;
   1 Peter 2:9-10).

And the natural response to this triad of truth? "To Him
be the glory and the dominion forever and ever. Amen"
(Revelation 1:6). As we reflect on our great sin and our
greater salvation, this should always produce in us a
depth of gratitude leading to praise and the exaltation
of our amazing God. Anything less is unworthy of him;
this kind of grateful worship is what he deserves.

Jesus Is Returning (Revelation 1:7)—John now calls to mind Daniel's prophecy of Messiah's second coming. "Behold, He is coming
with the clouds" (cf. Daniel 7:13). This prophecy, which is described
in much greater detail in Revelation 19, is sharply contrasted with not
only Christ's first coming, but also with his appearance at the rapture
of the church. At his incarnation, Jesus came to bring redemption.
At the rapture, he will come to rescue his bride from the tribulation
judgments (1 Thessalonians 1:10; 4:13-18; 5:9; 2 Thessalonians 2:6-7;

Revelation 3:10). And as he bursts through the clouds over Israel at the conclusion of the seven-year tribulation, he comes bringing retribution and wrath to his enemies (Matthew 24:36-41; Revelation 19:11-21). Redemption. Rescue. Retribution.

But verse 7 here is speaking specifically about his second coming—his final appearance in the sky. And unlike the rapture experience, during which only believers will see him, here, "every eye will see Him" (verse 7). The second coming will be a dramatic global event, one witnessed by every living soul on planet Earth at that time. And in contrast to the rapture, where his return is welcomed, those billions who witness his second coming will experience great terror and dread.

Jesus Is Renown (Revelation 1:8)—John concludes his salutary remarks with a quote from the triune God: "'I am the Alpha and the Omega,' says the Lord God, 'who is and who was and who is to come, the Almighty.'"

Alpha is the first letter of the Greek alphabet, and *Omega* the last. Here, God is claiming to be the sum total of all that there is, the consummation of knowledge and wisdom (Colossians 1:15-16). There is no one who existed before our God, and no one will outlast him. He has always been. Self-existent. Self-sustaining. Self-sufficient. Independent. The eternal sovereign. The one who is guaranteed to come again. He is saying, "I am the point of history and humanity, the very reason for your existence" (see Colossians 1:15-18). He is preeminent and all-encompassing.

It's as if he is proclaiming, "Church…what you are about to see in Revelation? I got this. It is I who will do this!"

Jesus Is Revealing (Revelation 1:9-11)—Now John, the beloved disciple, identifies himself with the believers to whom he is writing, letting them know that he, too, is a "fellow partaker in the tribulation and kingdom and perseverance which are in Jesus." Like those late first-century Christians, John was also suffering under the Roman emperor Domitian (AD 81–96). Specifically, he had been banished to

Patmos, a small island in the Aegean Sea off the coast of Asia Minor (modern-day Turkey).

Patmos is a rocky island, about ten miles long and six miles wide, and it was barren in John's day. This made it the perfect location for a Roman penal colony, like an ancient "Alcatraz of the Aegean Sea." John was there not because he had committed some heinous crime, but "because of the word of God in the testimony of Jesus" (verse 9; see 2 Timothy 2:8-10; 3:11-12).

While in solitude on a Sunday (the Lord's day), John found himself "in the Spirit" (Revelation 1:10). This refers to a unique and powerful filling of the Holy Spirit that can signify either direct revelation from God or even a trance-like vision involving the same (Matthew 22:43; Acts 10:10; Revelation 4:2). Biblical visions are like dreams, only the person is awake and the experience even more real. All past biblical visions were validated by the prophets or apostles. Many today claim similar yet unbiblical and unsubstantiated dreams and visions, and Scripture warns us to ignore such pretenders and counterfeits (Ezekiel 13:3, 6, 9-10; Jeremiah 23:16; Matthew 7:15-20; 2 Corinthians 11:13-15; Jude 12-13).

The Voice

John's vision of Christ did not result in a literary contract or movie deal, but rather, a book of inspired Scripture! In his vision, he hears behind him a voice "like the sound of a trumpet" (Revelation 1:10). The voice issued a simple mandate: "Write in a book what you see, and send it to the seven churches" (verse 11). John will hear this command to "write" a total of 12 times in Revelation.[4] And the book he will write is Revelation itself.

However, John is completely unprepared for what happens next. Now, fully immersed in the vision, he discovers the voice to be that of Jesus Christ himself (verse 12). He sees Christ standing in the middle of seven golden lampstands, a symbolic representation of the seven churches that would receive this book (verse 20). Since seven is the number of completeness, the seven lampstands are interpreted by many Bible scholars to represent all the churches, both then and now.

What stuns John is that the Jesus he sees here is an unfamiliar one, even to him. You may recall that John had heard the voice of Christ before. He had also seen and touched him during his earthly ministry (1 John 1:1). He had even spent 40 days with Christ while he was in his post-resurrection body (John 20:19-25, 30; 21:24; Acts 1:6-11). However, he had not yet seen the *glorified* Christ. *This* Jesus was no longer speaking in parables, healing the sick, and passing out bread and fish to the multitudes. His "work" the Father had sent him to accomplish had long been completed (John 4:34; 6:38-39). His days as the suffering Savior were over. He is now the exalted one, enthroned above, glorified and prepared to pour out unimaginable wrath on humanity and planet Earth.

In obedience to the command in Revelation 1:11, John picks up his quill, and with no doubt a trembling hand, begins to write what he sees. Here, then, is the portrait of the Revelation Christ he paints for us.

He Is Righteous (Revelation 1:13)—John sees Jesus as one "like a son of man." This is the term Christ used most often in the Gospels to describe himself (81 times). Referencing Daniel 7:13, it speaks of his uniqueness as the God-man, of deity incarnated, and the fact that he was unexplainably and simultaneously 100 percent man, yet also 100 percent God.

Jesus is clothed with a "robe reaching to the feet" (Revelation 1:13). In the earliest Greek translation of the Old Testament (known as the Septuagint, or LXX), this word "robe" was mostly used to describe the garment of the high priest. The "golden sash" across his chest likely pictures his role as our high priest, representing us before the Father (cf. Leviticus 16:1-4; Hebrews 2:17; 3:1; 4:14; 5:5).

John next notices Jesus' head and hair, which were "white like white wool, like snow" (Revelation 1:14). The emphasis here is not on the color white per se, but on the brightness and brilliance. We may talk about "white light" in light bulbs, but we also speak in terms of wattage, or lumens. John is portraying Christ's luminescence, or the brilliance of the light glowing around his head. It no doubt reminded the apostle of Daniel's similar vision of the Ancient of Days: "His vesture was like white snow, and the hair of His head like pure wool" (Daniel 7:9).

Scripture calls a gray head a "crown of glory" (Proverbs 16:31). And Jesus certainly is the sum total of all knowledge and wisdom, as we saw back in verse 8. But here, this is more likely a direct reference to the brilliance of his holiness (cf. Exodus 33:9-20).

A third aspect of Jesus' righteousness is seen in his eyes, described here as being "like a flame of fire" (Revelation 1:14). This speaks of the power and depth of his penetrating gaze. He sees it all—open or hidden, known or secret. This includes deeds, thoughts, and even motives (Luke 12:3; 1 Corinthians 3:13; 4:5).

Several years ago, I was honored to write the autobiography of Dr. Raymond Damadian, the brilliant medical genius who conceived of and invented the MRI machine. While working with Dr. Damadian, I learned that MRI technology can see things that are hidden from X-rays and even CT scans. It permeates through bone and muscle, detecting everything from herniated discs to pinched nerves to spinal tumors. That's better than Superman's X-ray vision. Like an MRI, Jesus' vision sees into the deepest part of humanity to diagnose and declare the truth about us. It is with these same flaming eyes that he will also examine the churches (Revelation 2:18) and judge the lost at his second coming (19:12).

He Is Refining (Revelation 1:15)—John's gaze turns to Jesus' feet, which are like burnished bronze. This phrase (one word in the Greek text) appears nowhere else in Greek literature outside of here and in Revelation 2:18. Most believe it has to do with the bronze being bright or polished, and here specifically, a bronze that is glowing due to being heated up in a furnace. In Exodus 38:1-8, we read of the tabernacle altar, which was covered in bronze. When heated up, like other metals, it would glow. The Jesus who stands before John is the refining, purifying judge.

He Is Reproving (Revelation 1:15)—Previously, John heard the Son of Man's voice "like the sound of a trumpet" (verse 10). But now that changes to "the sound of many waters." Being exiled on the rocky Isle of Patmos, the sound of waves crashing against the shore would've been familiar to the aged disciple. A trumpet was used to call armies to attention, or to announce the arrival of the Roman dignitary, such as a conquering general returning from battle. In the Old Testament, a shofar (a trumpet made from a ram's horn) was blown to gather the people of God together, and also to call soldiers to war. In the context of these verses, this trumpet-like voice is probably intended to arrest John's attention. And it was a voice he would surely recognize (John 10:4-5, 27-28).

Now that Jesus has John's attention, his voice conveys the commanding authority of God himself. In the right hand of the authoritative Christ are "seven stars," which verse 20 interprets for us to be the seven messengers of the churches in Revelation 2–3. Though some see these to be special angels (Greek *angelos* = "messengers"), it is better to view them as the pastors of the churches in Asia Minor. Pastors are charged with shining the truth of God's Word to the people of God. But nowhere in Scripture do we see angels being given responsibility over individual congregations. Pastors are God's primary spokesmen to his people (see Ephesians 4:11-17), and Jesus holds these pastors in his right hand (the strong hand, or hand of authority), protecting them.

Next, John sees coming out of Jesus' mouth "a sharp two-edged sword" (Revelation 1:16). The author of Hebrews portrayed the Word of God as such a sword (Hebrews 4:12). There are two Greek words translated "sword" in the New Testament—*macharia* (Hebrews 4:12), and *rhomphaia* (a long, broad sword), which is more like a *Braveheart* sword. The latter is the word used here, and also in Revelation 19:15. At Armageddon, Christ will arrive to judge and slaughter millions with that sword. But here in Revelation 1, he is preparing to perform surgery on his churches. Jesus' words are about to cut into the seven congregations, opening up their collective hearts for the purpose of healing and restoring them. His word will reveal what's really going on inside the body of Christ in their respective churches.

Jesus' word is also doing that today through those pastor-teachers who are faithful to preach the Word, even when it is not popular to do so. And their diligence is needed more critically now than perhaps at any other time in church history. For in these last days, many are departing from the faith, paying attention to myths, doctrines of demons, and delivering ear tickling, self-help sermons (1 Timothy 4:1-2; 2 Timothy 4:1-5).

He Is Radiating (Revelation 1:16)—John sees Jesus' face "like the shining sun in its strength." This no doubt is the radiance of his majestic glory. The author of Hebrews echoes this portrait of Christ, describing "the radiance of His glory and the exact representation of His nature" (1:3).

Have you ever attempted to look directly into the sun? Maybe *once*, right? It's not recommended, as the brilliance emanating from the sun overwhelms our eyes' ability to process such light. Even a quick glance upward will cause you to squint and immediately look away. That's because the ultraviolet light from the sun can damage your cornea and even cause blindness in as little as a few seconds. But the sun is just a star, one of hundreds of billions spoken into existence by the creator Jesus (John 1:1-3; see also Genesis 1:14-19; Colossians 1:16). Those heavenly bodies broadcast the glory of God through what has been made (Psalm 19:1). But his radiance is beyond even that of the sun and stars above. This kind of glory is intrinsic in God, seen here in the face of the Son. John must have recoiled as he beheld the brilliance of this glorious Christ. The apostle isn't merely learning a theological truth or simply gaining more knowledge about Jesus. Far from an intellectual encounter, John here *experiences* this glory.[5]

He Is Revered (Revelation 1:17)—Periodically, someone claims to have either had a vision or have died and visited heaven. While there, they typically "meet and speak with Jesus." However, two glaring problems arise from such assertions.

1. The heaven they describe is different from what is portrayed in Scripture, and

2. Jesus always bears zero resemblance to the Christ we see here in Revelation 1.

What typically follows is a best-selling book marketed to gullible and undiscerning Christians worldwide.

John's encounter with Christ disagrees with these modern-day claims. And his experience initiates a vastly different response as well: "When I saw Him, I fell at His feet like a dead man" (verse 17).

While preaching on this passage a few years back, I highlighted the glaring contradictions between John's portrayal of Jesus and the supposed modern-day visits to heaven in which Jesus is said to appear. Afterward, a woman stormed over to my book table and began yelling at me, rebuking me for daring to question anyone's "personal experience with Christ." She went on to explain how she, too, had once "died and gone to heaven," and that everything I had said was wrong. Not wishing to exacerbate the situation, I attempted to diffuse her emotional outburst.

"Ma'am," I explained, "I am not doubting that you believe you had some sort of special experience. You are free to believe what you want. However, I'm simply saying that I don't accept any such stories as authoritative." But my statement that God's Word trumped her experience didn't go over well. She stormed off, declaring, "You are not a mature Christian!"

It's worth pointing out here that any experience that contradicts the Word of God cannot be *from* God, as he is not self-contradictory. Truth is what determines our experience, not vice versa. John was severely traumatized in body, mind, and spirit upon seeing this vision of Christ. His knees buckled. His body trembled, and his heart was humbled as he bowed at Jesus' feet. He would have experienced sensory overload, suffering from what we could call "the shock of holiness." His faculties went into shutdown mode. He was blown away. Devastated.

Daniel's encounter with an angel produced a similar experience (Daniel 10:8-9, 17). Isaiah, Ezekiel, and Paul were all traumatized by their visions of God (Isaiah 6:5; Ezekiel 1:28; Acts 26:13-14).

Put bluntly, seeing this Christ, whether in person (like John) or through Scripture (like us), should *wreck us.*

This is "experiencing God"!

If there is one message Jesus Christ wants us to take away after meeting him, it's this: He is God, and we are not.

Being in Jesus' presence should trigger a reverential fear that instantly causes us to see ourselves as we truly are: Human. Fallen. Frail. Unworthy. Ruined. *Sinners.*

The disciples, upon seeing Jesus control the forces of nature simply by speaking to the wind and the waves, "became *very much afraid* and said to one another, 'Who, then, is this, that even the wind and the sea obey Him?'" (Mark 4:39-41). And Jesus rebuked them for their fear of the storm and their lack of faith (verse 40).

To see Jesus is not a casual encounter, but rather, a catastrophic experience. And we must never forget this.

He Is Reassuring (Revelation 1:17)—Fortunately, Jesus does not leave John face down, paralyzed by fear. Instead, he lovingly lays his right hand on him, comforting him. And he says, "Do not be afraid."

But why not? After all that John had just seen and felt and experienced, why not just stay a "dead man"? I think one of the reasons is because Jesus had a special mission for John. A divine commission. Jesus wanted John to pick up a prophetic pen and "write the things which you have seen [past], and the things which are [present], and the things which will take place after these things [future]" (verse 19). This is essentially the outline of the book of Revelation.

John would go on to catalog the last-ever prophecy given before Jesus returns for his bride at the rapture. However, there are a few more comforting reasons that John had to look beyond the fear that had so suddenly shocked him into this near-death experience.

First, Jesus proclaimed himself to be "the first and the last" (verse 17). He would later remind the church at Smyrna of this truth (2:8). This was also among his last descriptions of himself in the closing verses of Revelation (22:13).

Jesus wrote the opening chapter of history (Genesis 1), and he will also close out his written revelation at the end of this book. But beyond this, it's a declaration of his deity too. An affirmation that he indeed is God, and "there is no other" (Isaiah 45:5). Second, he reminds John that he is "the living One; and I was dead, and behold, I am alive forevermore" (Revelation 1:18).

A dead Savior is a powerless one. It is as if Christ was saying to him, "John, see once again with your eyes that I am alive, just as you did after my resurrection."

Christ actually died. His substitutionary death for us on the cross accomplished our salvation. And his resurrection was absolute confirmation of that sacrificial payment for sin. Everything about Christianity stands or falls with the resurrection. It is the proof that the faith, *our* faith, is real (1 Corinthians 15:1-19).

And through his resurrection, Jesus defeated and conquered man's greatest enemy—death. He even reigns over hell, the place of *his* wrath, not the devil's (Revelation 14:9-11; see also 2 Corinthians

4:4). Jesus is also "alive forevermore" (Revelation 1:18), meaning he will never die again.

Is This the Christ I Know?

So, because Jesus is God, because he rose again, because he will never die again, and because he has conquered our worst enemy and is in charge of the future, John can now get up and get going on his special-ops mission for God.

And one more thing: Because this Jesus is a living, loving Lord, everything John has endured and done for him has been seen. Because Christ is alive, John's faith is validated and his sufferings are not in vain. Likewise, if you ever wonder whether it's all worth it—whether the struggles, the battles, the sufferings, and the sorrow will one day pay off—then Revelation 1:17-18 should settle the issue for you (cf. 1 Corinthians 15:58). Everything you do for God matters. It counts.

Our view of God determines everything about us. Therefore, Scripture's description of Christ must be what informs and influences our vision of Jesus. The questions we must ask ourselves are these: Is this the Christ I know? How can I encounter this Revelation Jesus and stay asleep? And how can I ever remain the same?

Perhaps now you're beginning to see why some people avoid Revelation!

CHAPTER 3

LETTERS TO THE CHURCHES THEN AND NOW, PART 1

The God Who *Reproves*

Revelation 2:1–3:22

Much of Revelation has to do with God's wrath poured out through a series of catastrophic judgments during the final seven years of human history. And we will take an in-depth look at each of those judgments in subsequent chapters. But we also know that those seven years also mark the 70th week of Daniel for the nation Israel (Daniel 9:24-27). It is in this final era that God will turn his attention back to the nation Israel, to spiritually restore her following centuries of a "partial hardening" (Romans 11:25-26). During this time, a Jewish remnant will turn to the Messiah for forgiveness and salvation (Zechariah 13:8-9). It will be a time of chastening that ultimately brings about the glorious salvation of national Israel (Jeremiah 30:7; 11:22-23; Daniel 12:1-10).

However, prior to these judgments on the earth and Israel's salvation, Jesus must first visit with his bride and purify her in preparation for his rapture return. I believe this rapture event will occur prior to the seven-year tribulation primarily, but not exhaustively, for the following reasons:

1. God's past pattern of deliverance before sending judgment. Historically, before divine wrath was poured out from heaven, God delivered his righteous servants, as illustrated in the examples of Noah, Lot, and Enoch (who was literally raptured to heaven) (Genesis 5:22; 7:10-13; 19:12-26).

2. Jesus promised to return and take his bride to his Father's house (John 14:1-3). This cannot refer to the second coming, because Scripture tells us the church will return *with* Christ *from* heaven (Revelation 19:7-9, 11-14).

3. Paul prophesied a pre-tribulational deliverance of the church (1 Thessalonians 1:10; 5:9). The details of this event are broken down in 1 Thessalonians 4:13-18. Eschatology was a doctrine already familiar to the Thessalonian believers when Paul wrote 2 Thessalonians 2:1-7, where he reminded them, "Do you not remember that when I was still with you, I was telling you these things?" (verse 5). Christians are never promised immunity from trials or persecution. In fact, both Jesus and Paul stated that this would be our experience here on earth because (1) we are not of this world, and Jesus "chose [us] out of the world" (John 15:18-21), and (2) all those who desire to live godly lives will suffer some form of persecution (2 Timothy 3:12).

Jesus also prophesied that "tribulation" would be a part of life for us while we're here on earth (John 16:33). However, we must also heed Scripture's clear distinction between *man's* wrath and *God's* wrath. On the cross, Jesus absorbed the full fury of God's anger toward us and our sin (2 Corinthians 5:21; see also Matthew 26:42; 27:46; John 19:30). As a result, when we place our faith in him for our salvation, we are declared righteous in his sight (Romans 5:1). Because of this, "there is now no condemnation for those who are in Christ Jesus" (Romans 8:1). This effectively means that God's anger toward us has been fully satisfied in Christ and his substitutionary sacrifice. There isn't even an ounce of wrath or judgment left for us. We are his children, his beloved.

As we will see in Revelation 6:1, when the tribulation judgments begin, it is the "Lamb" (Jesus) who breaks the seals and pours out God's righteous anger on planet Earth and its inhabitants. This is the official beginning of God's wrath during that time. Therefore, we must be delivered prior to this time, which means a *pre*-tribulational rapture.

4. The portrayal of the church in Revelation provides further evidence that we are absent during the tribulation. The word *church* is used 20 times in Revelation. Here is how it breaks down:

   - Chapters 1–3: 19 times
   - Chapter 22: 1 time
   - Chapters 6–19 (during the tribulation): zero times
   - Additionally, the church is portrayed as being *on earth* in

Revelation 2–3, and returning *with* Christ from heaven in chapter 19.

For these reasons and many more, we can conclude that Jesus' bride will be rescued from earth before the tribulation begins.[1]

I'd like to add one note of clarification here. In the time between now and the rapture deliverance, I do expect the church (true believers) to experience increasing marginalization, discrimination, persecution, and martyrdom. This is one reason we must take to heart Scripture's admonition to not forsake "our own assembling together," but to be "encouraging one another; and all the more as you see the day drawing near" (Hebrews 10:25-26). That said, Christ has some unfinished business with his beloved bride. She is in dire need of purification and preparation in these last days.

Jesus instructed John to "write in a book what you see, and send it to the seven churches [in Asia Minor]" (Revelation 1:11). Each of these churches, though literal and existing at the close of the first century, seem to represent the condition of the church throughout the past 2,000 years. In fact, though one cannot be dogmatic, it has been suggested by some scholars and commentators that each of the seven churches pictures the state of Christ's bride in successive periods of church history:

Ephesus—the early church to AD 100

Smyrna—the church suffering under pagan persecution, AD 100–313

Pergamum—paganism infiltrates the church, AD 500

Thyatira—papal dominance in the church, Dark Ages to the mid-1500s

Sardis—Protestant Reformation to the late 1700s

Philadelphia—the Great Awakening, the rebirth of biblical priority to the mid-1800s

Laodicea—the last-days church, lukewarm and complacent up to the time of the rapture

However, as we look back at church history, this historical and chronological comparison isn't the only avenue of application to our lives. Within each letter to the churches, we see similarities to the present-day bride of Christ as well. Jesus' words are effectively a "state of the church" address. Christ is simultaneously surveying the spiritual landscape while, at the same time, pausing to examine each church individually.

In the rest of this chapter, we're going to look through the lens of Scripture and see what Jesus sees concerning the church, both then and now. And as we observe these seven messages, we will notice a consistent pattern. In almost every letter, Jesus…

- reveals something about himself
- shares what he knows about the church
- gives a commendation
- delivers a rebuke
- provides counsel
- issues a warning
- offers a reward

Ephesus—You've Lost That Loving Feeling (2:1-7)

Ephesus was a thriving metropolis in the first century AD, with an estimated population of anywhere from 250,000 to 500,000. It was the largest city in the Roman province of Asia. And though it wasn't the capital, the governor's residence was there. Well-known athletic games were held there each year, and Ephesus's outdoor theater boasted a seating capacity of 25,000.

In AD 89, Ephesus became a temple warden for the Roman imperial cult, and a temple for Domitian (AD 81–96) was erected. This emperor preferred to be addressed as "dominus and deus"—lord and god. He was a harsh ruler and was eventually hated by most, including members of the Roman Senate, which, following his death, pronounced him to be what was later referred to as *damnatio memoriae* ("a condemnation of memory").[2] This pronouncement effectually erased his name from all public monuments, and statues of him were destroyed. This was the first century's version of "cancel culture."

It was at Ephesus that the Temple of Artemis (Greek name), or Diana (Roman name), resided. This temple was considered one of the seven wonders of the ancient world, being 425 feet long (nearly 2.5 football fields) and 220 feet wide, supported by 127 massive columns. Prostitutes populated the temple and were viewed as priestesses. To sleep with a temple prostitute was considered a sacred act of worship. In fact, the whole city was obsessed with Diana, a goddess of wild animals and the hunting of them (she was sometimes referred to as "Diana the Huntress"). But she was also considered a virgin goddess associated with fertility who aided women in conception and delivery. She was sometimes depicted as possessing a multitude of breasts, an allusion to her fertility-giving powers. There was even a month-long goddess festival in the spring.

In Acts 19, Paul spoke concerning how he authenticated his message about Christ with "extraordinary miracles" (verse 11). In Ephesus, he saw many people healed and divinely delivered from demonic control. In fact, so many were converting from witchcraft to Jesus that it greatly affected the Ephesian economy—people were burning their books on sorcery. Those who made idols and shrines to Artemis (Diana) ignited a riot against Paul, chanting, "Great is Artemis of the Ephesians!" This went on for two solid hours! (verse 34).

Paul had founded the Ephesian church on his second missionary journey (Acts 18), and when he returned to visit the believers there, he stayed for two years (Acts 19:10).

Fast-forward now about 40 years.

By the time John received the vision of Revelation (AD 95), the Ephesian church was hardly recognizable.

Jesus' Revelation (2:1)

He is "the One who holds the seven stars in His right hand, the One who walks among the seven golden lampstands." In Revelation 1:20, Jesus explains that the stars are "the angels of the seven churches" (literally, "messengers" or "pastors"). And he says the seven lampstands are the seven churches, which represent the light of Christ and his truth to the world.

Jesus' Declaration (2:2)

He recognizes the deeds, toil, and perseverance of the believers in Ephesus, acknowledging that they have worked hard and remained faithful, despite being surrounded by a pagan, immoral culture.

Jesus' Commendation (2:2-3)

This church did not tolerate evil people in the congregation. They were tough on sin, not an easy task in a city filled with blatant wickedness and idolatry. They also tested those who claimed to be apostles. In other words, they were sound in doctrine and spiritual discernment, keeping false teaching out of the assembly. Again, not an easy task considering their belief system made them part of a scant minority in Ephesus. They had not grown weary to the point of giving up.

These Christians had stood firm, doctrinally and morally. They had taken seriously Paul's final admonition to them upon his departure

(Acts 20:28-31). They hated "the deeds of the Nicolaitans," which Jesus also hated (2:6). We are not exactly sure who the Nicolaitans were, but they were some sort of offshoot sect. The name Nicolaitans may have come from any of the following:

1. *Nikao*, "to conquer," and *laos*, "the people." So it may refer to some type of domineering clerical hierarchy.

2. A licentious group advocating participation in pagan love feasts and free love.

3. Followers of Nicolas (Acts 6:5), a convert from Antioch.

But whatever the origin of the Nicolaitans, the Ephesian believers didn't put up with them or their teachings. They believed the right things. They guarded the truth. They were sound, steadfast, and faithful in service.

Jesus' Rebuke (2:4)

Jesus reprimanded the believers in Ephesus because they had "left their first love." Love for God remains the greatest commandment (Matthew 22:36-38). And while it is true that we cannot truly love God apart from the revelation of this truth, doctrine alone does not automatically produce a committed affection for him. Truth about God moves us to love him. And love for God should always precede our obedience to him (John 14:15). It is from this love that everything else we do for God flows. We work, serve, stand for truth, and persevere because we love him. To remove this love from the spiritual equation is to become a Christian version of the Pharisees. Without love, ultimately, nothing else matters.

It is the nature of people and the organizations they work in to deteriorate over time. Many of our founding universities in America, including Harvard and Princeton, were once citadels of biblical truth. But time and compromise eroded these schools' original commitment to God and his Word. Like churches, these institutions don't necessarily shut their doors after the passage of time. They just morph and redefine themselves for a new generation. The bride of Christ today is in danger of losing her distinctiveness, her vision, her pioneer spirit, and her feral nature. She has become tame and domesticated. She has gone from being a living organism to an *organization*. A business run like any other secular business.

This is how churches die.

Like the Ephesian church, we too, can, sustain programs, ministries, activities, outreaches, and religious services—all the while maintaining a certain air of spiritual respectability. But Jesus is looking for more than just doctrinal perseverance. He wants spiritual passion. He desires more than activity. He wants affection. He requires more than doctrine and duty. He wants devotion (Luke 10:38-42). Christ is looking for more than service and endurance. It is called, in his own words, "first love." Jesus' MRI on the church in Ephesus revealed a massive loss of radical, revolutionary love for the one who promises to return one day to earth.

How is first love lost over time? When…

- you fail to live with an awareness of your own depravity (Jeremiah 17:9; Romans 7:18).

- you lose the passion to worship and be with God's people (Hebrews 10:23-25).

- you've lost the gratitude of forgiveness (2 Peter 1:9; see also Romans 8:1).

- your hunger for experiencing the truth together wanes.

- you have knowledge without enthusiasm.

- you can gather together and not express love for Jesus.

- you cease to see lives changed.

- you no longer care to influence or tell others about the Lord.

Jesus' Counsel (2:5)

Christ's advice to the Ephesian pastor was to instruct his church to do three things in order to restore them to himself:

1. *Remember*—They were to "remember from where you have fallen." In other words, recall how it used to be in your relationship with Jesus. And what did that relationship once look like? From Paul's previous encounter with the Ephesians, we discover that...

   - they possessed a healthy fear of the power of Jesus and magnified his name (Acts 19:17).

   - their fervent love for the Lord and faith in him caused them to love one another more (Ephesians 1:15; see also Jeremiah 2:2-5).

   Jesus surely remembers what our relationship with him was like in the beginning. And as the old Christian adage goes, "If God feels far away from you, guess who moved?"

   Paul's letter to the Ephesians was one of the most positive, encouraging, and hope-filled epistles in the entire New Testament. So Jesus is essentially saying here, "Remember how it used to be? Remember how *we* used to be? Reflect on your salvation." The verb tense here indicates that they were to "keep on remembering"—to regularly recall how it first felt to be in love with him.

2. *Repent*—The word *repent* is made up of two Greek

words—*meta* (to change according to), and *noeo* (mind), so to repent is to "have a change of mind that results in a change of life." Their church was founded upon a solid foundation of repentance (see Acts 19:18-19). Repentance is more than just emotional sorrow or sadness over sin. It involves a conscious decision, an act of the will, a choice. Jesus' rebuke must therefore make a difference in their lives.

3. *Return*—"Do the deeds you did at first." And what were those deeds? They were actions inspired and motivated by their love for Jesus. This tells us that sometimes the way forward with God is to go back and revisit the old ways, to reintroduce yourself to the person you were when you first met Jesus. And deeds done for Christ are evidence of genuine repentance.

Jesus' Warning (2:5)

Christ guarantees that if the people in the Ephesian church fail to heed his counsel, he is "coming to you and will remove your lampstand out of its place—unless you repent." The lampstand represents the light, or influence for Christ, in their city. It should set off alarms in our soul to think that Jesus would no longer use us for his glory and kingdom. And if losing our spiritual influence is not enough to motivate our repentance, then we have for sure lost our first love.

Oh, to be a people madly in love with a God who is madly in love with us!

From the outside, things may look great in our churches—programs, people, service to the community. But Jesus' MRI goes past the external. Past the presentation of the music, drama, media, and even the message. His evaluation penetrates the collective heart of the body. He walks among his people and asks, "Does this church love me?"

"Do *you* love me?"

Jesus' Reward (2:7)

All Revelation's letters were meant for all the churches, indicating that we are to pay attention not only to our own church, but also to the state of the bride elsewhere in the world. But the promise Jesus makes to the Ephesian Christians is an invitation to "hear," or to pay close attention to what he is saying. The reward is as follows: "To him who overcomes, I will grant to eat of the tree of life which is in the Paradise of God."

Who is the one who overcomes? Elsewhere in Scripture, according to the same author, John, it is all true believers: "Whatever is born of God overcomes the world; and this is the victory that has overcome the world—our faith. Who is the one who overcomes the world, but he who believes that Jesus is the Son of God?" (1 John 5:4-5).

And what do all believers get? According to Jesus, access to the "tree of life." This tree was originally in the garden of Eden (Genesis 2:9; 3:22), and it represents the full enjoyment of eternal life—like supernatural vitamins. We see this tree again in Revelation 22:2, 14, 19, in the new heaven, our eternal home.

Smyrna—Suffering for Jesus (Revelation 2:8-11)

The word *Smyrna* means "myrrh," which was a sweet perfume used for embalming. In the Old Testament, it was also used to describe the fragrance of a bridegroom (Psalm 45:8; Song of Solomon 3:6). Today it is the city of Izmir, Turkey. Only a few days' journey north on foot from Ephesus, Smyrna was known for its beauty and charm. There were coins engraved that read "First of Asia in beauty and size." It was called the "glory of Asia" because of its planned developments, beautiful temples, and ideal harbor. At the time of John's writing, Smyrna had a population of nearly 200,000 people. Considered a wealthy city, it was also the birthplace of the Greek author and poet Homer.

The church began either when the Jews returned there after Pentecost (Acts 2), or during Paul's missionary journey to Ephesus (Acts 19). However, here in Revelation 2 is the only place it's mentioned in Scripture. Interestingly, what is believed to be the earliest Christian "graffiti" has been found at Smyrna—*ho dedokos pneuma* = "the one who has given the Spirit" (i.e., Jesus).

Jesus' Revelation (2:8)

Jesus announces himself as "the first and the last, who was dead, and has come to life." He is the eternal one who has conquered death.

Jesus' Declaration (2:9)

Jesus says to the believers in Smyrna, "I know what you're going through." He acknowledges three areas of struggle they were facing:

1. Tribulation (Greek *thlipsis*)—This means to be under enormous pressure. These believers were under a lot of stress, and things were about to get worse for them.

2. Poverty—Jesus doesn't use the ordinary word to describe being poor, but one that signifies abject poverty, like that of a beggar (probably due to being labelled as outcasts and marginalized in a pagan culture). And yet Jesus tells them, in his estimation, "You are rich." They had every reason to fail, but they didn't because they had everything they needed in Christ. The church in Smyrna was small—it wasn't influential or powerful. We tend to think wealthy megachurches are the ones Christ blesses. But bigger

is by no means automatically better in God's kingdom. Approximately 70 percent of churches in America have less than 100 members, and in 2020, an average-size congregation in the US was just 65 people.[3]

3. Slander—This came primarily from the Jews, who had distanced themselves from the Christians in order to avoid persecution. Jewish leaders officially excommunicated Christians as heretics sometime during the AD 80s to deflect attention from themselves. Emperor Domitian had passed a law requiring all people to worship him. But the Jews were considered exempt because of *religio licita*— "approved religion." Due to Judaism's great antiquity, their ancestral traditions were regarded as a source of social and political stability. So, the Jews there "slandered" the Christians (many of whom were also Jews!) to the Roman authorities in order to label them as "lawbreakers." As a result, believers were branded as rebels because they refused to worship the emperor. They would not participate in pagan religious ceremonies and some social life activities (those that revolved around pagan rituals or the emperor cult). And because they refused to worship the Roman gods, they were denounced as "atheists." The early Christians also faced accusations of cannibalism (the Lord's supper), immorality (a holy kiss), and political disloyalty (refusing to honor Caesar), and even incest (love for your brother and sister).

Because of all these troubles, the church was impoverished. Many Christians lost their jobs and had their property destroyed. The Jews poisoned public opinion against Christians, earning them the nickname "a synagogue of Satan" (i.e., acting just as Satan would against believers, see John 8:44).

Jesus' Rebuke

The Christian church at Smyrna received no rebuke from Jesus.

Jesus' Counsel (2:10)

Jesus said, "Do not fear what you are about to suffer." That is, "Stop being afraid." Christ let them know that tough times were on the way. For them, there would be a rocky road ahead.

Today, believers are persecuted for their faith, even in this very city of Smyrna (Izmir). And Christians in some 70 countries today are being beaten, burned, beheaded, imprisoned, relocated, and brutally murdered—just for trusting in Jesus.[4] Some believers in America have already suffered the loss of their businesses and become subject to cancel culture. And it is likely that more severe suffering is headed our way.

With the continued rise of immorality, lawlessness, and a climate of division and hate, our culture continues turning against Judeo-Christian values, even demonizing them. In a society sliding headlong toward Sodom, you can expect an ever-increasing rise in opposition to Christian beliefs and values, with believers becoming the targets of hate, discrimination, marginalization, and persecution. You may suffer for your faith—losing a promotion, sales, or being slandered and ridiculed for believing in Jesus. Don't be surprised when this happens, and know that (1) Jesus is always with you (Matthew 28:20), and (2) opposition is to be expected for all disciples (John 15:18-21). Also, (3) persecution is a test and an affirmation of the validity of your faith (Mark 8:38). Remember that Satan, the accuser, has no authority over you or your life (Psalm 56:11; Revelation 12:10).

Jesus' Promise (2:10-11)

Christ makes two promises to the believers in Smyrna:

1. The ones who are faithful will receive the "crown of life" (2:10; James 1:12).[5]

2. He who overcomes will not be hurt by the second death (2:11).

For this church, persecution was indeed on the way. In fact, some in the body of Christ were about to be arrested and thrown into prison for "ten days" (verse 10). This testing of their faith would produce endurance, which would contribute toward their maturity and completeness in Christ (James 1:2-4). Jesus' exhortation for them was to be faithful unto death or until the time of their departure from this earth. And the reason this prospect of death should not disturb them was because Jesus himself had already conquered death (Revelation 2:8). Because he lives, so will they.

The church at Smyrna teaches us that our power comes not from great influence, but rather, from having a strong relationship with Jesus. The devil persecutes believers in all ages of church history. But Christ knows what we're going through, and he is with us always, even to the end of the age (Matthew 28:20).

Pergamum—the Compromising Church (2:12-17)

Pergamum was the capital of Asia Minor for 250 years, and it was there that parchment paper was first widely used. The city boasted a huge library (200,000 volumes, which was later sent as a gift from Antony to Cleopatra). It was also a major center for pagan cults, and the first city to build a temple to Caesar (29 BC, Augustus). Therefore, it became the capital of the cult of Caesar worship.

The chief goddess of Pergamum was Athena, the Greek virgin goddess of reason, intelligent activity, the arts, and literature. In Greek mythology, Athena was the daughter of Zeus, the god of the sky and the chief Greek deity.

The people in Pergamum also worshipped Asklepios, the god of healing, which combined medicine with superstition and included the practice of having snakes slither all over a person (cf. Genesis 3:1-3, where Satan is personified as a serpent). During the reign of Diocletian (284–305), Christian stonecutters were executed for refusing to carve the image of Asklepios.

Finally, another chief deity honored in Pergamum was Bacchus, the god of drunkenness. And on the Acropolis was also a huge, throne-shaped altar to Zeus.

Jesus' Revelation (2:12)

Christ describes himself as "the One who has the sharp two-edged sword" (verse 12). Unlike the dagger-like sword depicted in Hebrews 4:12 and Ephesians 6:17, the sword here again is *rhomphaia*, meaning a large, broad sword, often used by those on horseback (also mentioned in Luke 2:35; Revelation 2:16; 6:4; 19:15, 21). This was the first clue to the believers in Pergamum that Christ's message was not likely to be a friendly or pleasant one.

Jesus' Declaration (2:13)

Jesus said, "I know where you dwell, where Satan's throne is." The phrase "Satan's throne" referred to either the Roman emperor or to Zeus, the god of the sky and ruler of the Olympian gods, and this may have been a reference to the Temple of Zeus in Pergamum.

Jesus' Commendation (2:13)

The Lord mentions Antipas (verse 13), a name that means "against all." We don't know exactly who he was; he may have been the pastor of the church there. But we do know he was either the first believer to die for his faith in Pergamum, or at least the most notable one. Jesus calls him "My *witness*," which, translated from the Greek, gives us the word *martyr*. Tradition says Antipas was cooked alive inside a brass bull. In this passage, he is immortalized for his martyrdom.

So many believers in the first century were killed for their faith in Christ that the word *witness* came to mean one who died for his faith in Christ. That would make people think twice before wanting to be a witness for Christ!

Jesus' Rebuke (2:14)

In spite of this congregation's orthodoxy and sacrifice, the Lord still had a list of grievances against those in the Pergamum church. Some people in their midst held to the "teaching of Balaam." In Numbers, Balaam prostituted his prophetic gift by unsuccessfully cursing Israel in exchange for money offered to him by Balak, king of Moab. He devised a plan to have Moabite women seduce Israeli men. The result was unions that led to all kinds of immorality (2 Corinthians 6:14-17) and idolatrous feasts (Numbers 22–25).

Coupled with this heresy were also those who followed the teaching of the "Nicolaitans," whom we saw condemned by the believers in the church at Ephesus.

Jesus' Counsel (2:16)

Jesus boldly told the people in the church at Pergamum to "repent," or to turn away from their sin. This is Christ using that "sword" mentioned in verse 12. Biblical repentance speaks of a change of mind or perspective that leads to an altered lifestyle. Then, like today, worldly philosophies and errant theology can creep into the church, diluting the gospel and derailing believers in their pursuit of Christlikeness. This is often done through redefining long-held biblical doctrines in order to accommodate the ever-devolving values of a decadent and depraved culture. The end result is that the church is no longer the church (Greek *ecclesia*, "called out ones"). When unbiblical thinking and living persists in believers or churches, they must be "called out" regarding their sin, which is what Christ does next.

Jesus' Warning (2:16)

"Repent, or else I am coming to you quickly, and I will make war against them with the sword of my mouth." (There's that long sword again.) Tolerance today is touted as one of society's highest and most admired virtues. But for Jesus' church, there are things about which we must exercise firm *in*tolerance. The Lord is effectively saying, "Read my lips. Do not tolerate them or their teaching in my church. Period. Confront them. Get rid of them and their beliefs and practices."

And he is serious.

Jesus "coming to" them is not a reference to the rapture, but rather, to some divine visitation of judgment. This "war" Christ promises likely involves some form of harsh discipline (possibly sickness, pestilence, or even death, as we'll see in 2:20-23).

Jesus' Promise (2:17)

To those who listen, and then overcome, Jesus pledges three rewards:

1. Hidden Manna—After the Jewish people left Egypt, manna was the literal nourishment God gave to them during their long desert journey. And in John 6:48-51, Jesus says he is our "hidden manna" that sustains us.

2. White Stone—This could refer to jurists casting a white stone when voting for a "not guilty" verdict for an accused person, or it may signify the promise of acceptance in heaven. Jesus could also be referring to the custom of a white stone being given to an athlete, on which the athlete's name was inscribed, to be used as

a ticket so that he could attend the victor's celebration banquet.

3. A New Name—Related to the white stone, this could be a special name reflecting the character of the one who overcame for the sake of Christ. This name is unknown until it is given.

Today, we live in a pagan world filled with thousands of gods that compete for our loyalty, allegiance, and worship. And they are all unfriendly to the exclusivity of the Lord Jesus Christ.

The believers in Smyrna were persecuted yet persevering. And there was no rebuke or condemnation for them. But the believers in Pergamum were residing in a difficult place and involved in compromise.

As back then, Jesus is asking us today: "Who's listening? Who's desperate for me? Who's seeking? Who's overcoming? Who's persevering?"

Thyatira—the Tolerant Church (2:18-19)

Thyatira was a Roman outpost established by Alexander the Great. This outpost guarded Pergamum. There was also a military academy there in third century AD, a sort of "West Point" of that day. The city was known for its purple dye, cloth goods, and trade guilds.

The gospel was likely brought there through Lydia, who was converted under Paul's ministry (Acts 16:14-15). God chose her to become the very first European Christian.

Jesus' message to Thyatira runs 12 verses and is the longest of the seven letters he sent to the churches in Asia Minor.

Jesus' Revelation (2:18)

Jesus introduces himself to the congregation at Thyatira as the "Son of God," reminding the readers who is sending the message. His eyes are like a flame of fire (i.e., he *sees*). In other words, Jesus is about to closely examine this church. His feet are like burnished bronze. As we saw in Revelation 1:15, this likely refers to him standing in judgment over them. Christ is revealing his authority and appealing to their respect for him.

Jesus' Declaration and Commendation (2:19)

Jesus told these believers, "I know your deeds." This church possessed many admirable qualities. They were marked by love, faith, service, and perseverance. They were growing in the quality and quantity of their good and godly deeds.

Jesus' Rebuke (2:20)

But then Jesus added, "I have this against you, that you tolerate the woman Jezebel." This woman was apparently a false prophetess who taught heresy and led Jesus' servants astray. In 1 Kings 16:31-33, we read about how Queen Jezebel corrupted her husband, combining the worship of God with that of Baal. Her name became synonymous with corruption, immorality, and idolatry. And her end was not a good one (2 Kings 9:30-37).

It is possible this woman had already violated God's divine order by assuming the role of teacher in the church (1 Timothy 2:11-15). It is also likely that this self-proclaimed prophetess encouraged loose living, sexual immorality, and a callousness toward offending weak and young Christians.

The believers in Thyatira were tolerant but had to be reminded that it is always a sin to tolerate sin. Earlier, Jesus had said that for those who lead young believers astray, it would be better that a "heavy millstone [be] hung around his neck," and that he be "drowned in the depth of the sea" (Matthew 18:6). In other words, such a person would be better off dead than to be allowed to mislead others.

Jesus then described the two ways Jezebel was corrupting the believers at Thyatira:

1. She led them to "commit acts of immorality"—In that

culture, after people ate dinner on their reclining beds, some would indulge in immoral acts on the same beds.

2. She led them to "eat things sacrificed to idols"—Though it was common to eat such food, it was often linked to immorality as well. Weak or young Christians can't distinguish between good and evil in the same way mature believers can (1 Corinthians 8:1-13). Newer Christians have little discernment. Like little children, they think in concrete terms—black and white, right and wrong. They're very specific in their obedience, and this can sometimes lead to legalism. Sometimes you can't say to a young believer, "Just use wisdom and biblical judgment" in the same way you can't tell a four-year-old to walk to the grocery store alone. They just aren't ready yet. And this false prophetess was acting like a spiritual predator, preying on the weaknesses of these young believers.

Jesus' Counsel (2:25)

Our Lord tells the Christians in this community to "hold fast until I come." This may be the first reference to the rapture in Revelation.

Jesus' Warning (2:21-23)

1. To Jezebel—He had given her time to repent, but she did not want to (verses 22-23). Therefore, Christ would "throw her on a bed of sickness." Translated: On a bed she sinned. Therefore, on a bed she will suffer. Whatever sickness this was, it was a serious and perhaps deadly one.

2. Those who followed her—All kinds of trouble (tribulation) would come their way (verses 22-23). This meant they would become very ill and even be killed by the "pestilence" Jesus sent to their bodies.

And why would he do this? To serve as an example and a warning to all the other churches, so they would know that it is he who "searches the minds and hearts," and "will give to each one of you according to your deeds." Jesus rewards according to what we *do*, not just what we say we believe or intend to do.

3. To the rest of the church—To those who haven't known "the deep things of Satan" (cf. 1 Corinthians 2:10—the deep things of God), he places no burden on them. Those erring church members may have rationalized that the only way to understand the "deep things of Satan" was to participate in the satanic acts. By doing so, they believed they would be better equipped to help others who were caught up in those things. This was probably a form of Christian gnosticism that believed the body was evil, while the spirit was good. Such errant thinking taught that it doesn't really matter what you do with your body, but rather, only your spirit.

Jesus' Promise (2:26-29)

Jesus says that those who overcome will reign with him in his millennial kingdom (verses 25-26), having "authority over the nations" (quoting Psalm 2:8). It is then and there that Jesus will "rule" the nations (verse 27; 19:15).

He also promises to "give him [the one who overcomes] the morning star" (verse 28; 22:16; 2 Peter 1:19). This is probably a reference to Christ himself, or a special fullness of relationship, experience, and intimacy with him in heaven.

Verse 29 ends with the admonition to pay close attention to what the Spirit says to the churches, meaning, "Do not ignore this message, but hear it and act upon it."

History records that the church in Thyatira eventually fell to the Montanist heresy that arose during the second century AD. Montanus believed God spoke to him directly, and that he could see Jesus. He claimed to have fresh revelation for the church apart from the Scriptures and apostles' writings. He was especially popular among women, two of whom were colleagues of his: Prisca (sometimes called Priscilla) and Maximilla, who also claimed to receive special inspiration from the Holy Spirit. Their popularity exceeded Montanus' own. "The Three," as they were known, spoke in ecstatic visions and urged their followers to fast and to pray, so that they might share in these revelations. They were all condemned as heretics and expelled from the church.

As you can see, Jesus is direct, thorough, and authoritative in his evaluation of the churches so far. He does this because he deeply loves his children (Hebrews 12:4-13). God's discipline is not condemnation, but rather, an effort toward *restoration*. Remember, Jesus' motivation is to prepare his bride prior to his return for her. He wants her to be pure and prepared for the day of consummation and consecration. When we see his chastising through this lens, it motivates us as well to freshly welcome his words to the churches and take them to heart for our own lives. By doing this, we are able to look back on our lives with few regrets and look forward to many rewards from our Savior and Lord!

CHAPTER 4

LETTERS TO THE CHURCHES THEN AND NOW, PART 2

The God Who *Reproves*

Revelation 2:1–3:22

So far, we've looked at four of the letters Christ sent to the seven churches in Asia Minor. Now let's look at the last three, as Jesus completes his internal audit of his church.

Sardis—The Dead Church (Revelation 3:1-6)

Sardis was a city that once served as the western capital of the Seleucid Empire (281–190 BC). In 133 BC, it became part of the Roman province of Asia. Sardis had a famous king named Croesus, who was so wealthy that a proverb was written of him. If you were describing someone as being fabulously wealthy, you said they were "as rich as Croesus."

The city was also known for its textile, dye, and gold industries.

Gold and silver coins were first minted in Sardis, and Aesop (Aesop's Fables) is rumored to have been from Sardis.

The city itself was perched 1,500 feet above the valley floor, and as such, was a fortress of sorts. History tells us it was conquered twice. The first time was when King Cyrus of Persia took the city in 549 BC after his army scaled the cliffs in the dark of night. Then again in 214 BC, Antiochus the Great did the same, as only one approach to the city was being guarded. Both times, the city's capture was due to overconfidence and a failure to keep watch for enemies.

Several centuries after being conquered, in the apostle John's day, the saying "to capture the acropolis of Sardis" was a proverb equated with doing the impossible. So impregnable was the city that it is said that a child could have defended it.

Sardis was later destroyed by an earthquake in AD 17 and rebuilt with aid from Tiberius Caesar. The nearby hot springs were so therapeutic it was said they could even give life to the dead.

An ancient Jewish synagogue was discovered in Sardis and is the largest one found outside of Israel.

Paul probably founded the church in Sardis as an outreach of Ephesus (Acts 19:10). However, by AD 95, Sardis was in a period of decline, though still somewhat prosperous.

Jesus' Revelation (3:1)

Christ describes himself to the church at Sardis as "the one who has the seven spirits." This is a reference to the Holy Spirit, either signifying his perfection or pointing back to Isaiah 11:2, where we read this about the Messiah:

> The Spirit of the LORD will rest on Him,
> The spirit of *wisdom* and *understanding*,
> The spirit of *counsel* and *strength*,
> The spirit of *knowledge* and the *fear* of the LORD.

We do know that, during the church age, Jesus is represented to the church through the Holy Spirit (John 14:16-17, 26; Acts 1:8; 2:1-4). He also is the one who has the "seven stars," or the seven pastors of the churches in Revelation 2–3 (cf. 1:20).

Jesus' Declaration (3:1b)

Jesus said, "I know your deeds." Unfortunately, this church is all but devoid of the Spirit. Though it had a name and reputation for being alive, it was spiritually dead.

Jesus' Commendation (3:1, 4)

Christ did acknowledge their "deeds," but there is almost no *commendation* for those deeds. There was a remnant, however, of a "few people in Sardis who have not soiled their garments; and they will walk with Me in white, for they are worthy" (verse 4).

So not everyone in the church was "dead." The word "soiled" means to be stained, defiled, smeared, or polluted—like an ink stain on a white shirt. In Scripture, garments often represent character and spiritual integrity (Isaiah 64:6; Jude 23; Ephesians 4:22, 24). This godly remnant had managed to avoid sliding into a spiritual coma and becoming part of the "walking dead" that comprised the rest of their fellow church members.

The phrase "walk with Me in white" refers to their purity of heart and deeds done for Christ. They had walked worthy of the Lord and would join him in the wedding celebration in heaven (Ephesians 4:1; Revelation 19:7-9).

Jesus' Rebuke (3:1)

There is no mention of any persecution against this church in this very pagan city. After all, why would Satan need to persecute a dead, ineffective church? Even so, the surrounding culture may have been a contributing factor to the church's downfall. This church had leaves, but no fruit (Matthew 21:19). They had form, but not life. They were open for business, but with no spiritual revenue to show for it.

William Barclay reportedly said, "A church is in danger when it begins to worship its own past."[1] Perhaps that was the case with this church. Today, there are many churches. But how many of them are truly alive? With that in mind, here are a few signs that a church may be dead or dying:

- a dependence on human effort and planning rather than on the Holy Spirit

- a calendar filled with activities but members not filled with the Holy Spirit

- run like a corporation or business rather than by faith, the Holy Spirit, and the Bible

- managers, charismatic personalities, and directional leaders are hired, but not God-called and biblically qualified pastors and teachers

- outreach to the community is preferred and prioritized over investing spiritual resources in its own members

- obsession with physical or numerical growth over biblical depth

- lay elders and leaders are primarily wealthy and influential businessmen instead of men full of faith and the Holy Spirit

- land acquisitions and building programs overshadow making disciples

- rests on past achievements and reputation

- avoids confronting cultural and moral evils from the pulpit

- presents personal development, self-improvement, and social issues over preaching the Word of God

It used to be that a dead church was primarily defined by boring liturgy and lack of emotion. Today, a dead church can be one that appears lively, or even has the word *life* in its name. It's a church that tries way too hard to persuade the world to like it. It pursues popularity and acceptance from culture rather than approval from God. A dead church goes through the motions, putting on elaborate Sunday morning services. Their focus is on *doing* church, not *being* the church.

And Jesus says that's unacceptable to him.

Like Samson, a dead church does not know that the Lord has departed from it (Judges 16:16-20). They still possess the same name and host the same activities. But the Holy Spirit's power is not present.

Jesus' Counsel (3:2-3)

There was a lot "broken" about this church, so there was a lot of divine counsel required.

Jesus tells the church at Sardis to do the following:

1. "Wake up" (verse 2)—They needed to open their eyes and see the Jesus of Revelation 1:12-18. "Wake up, stay up, be watchful and vigilant (*unlike* your city and its history!)." In order for those who are dead to respond to God, they must first be awakened. They must be spiritually awakened from their slumber and lethargy and become alert.

2. "Strengthen the things that remain" (verse 2)—Jesus wanted the people to strengthen what few spiritual embers were still burning and fan them into a mighty flame for God. Christ's reasoning? "For I have *not* found your deeds completed in the sight of My God" (verse 2).

3. "Remember what you received and heard" (verse 3)—
   Jesus wanted them to think back on the fundamental
   truths that once formed the foundation of the church
   and the people's faith. Part of what robs us of our
   spiritual dynamic is forgetting what brought us to
   Christ in the first place, including a realization of our
   sinful condition and our need for salvation. We need
   to recall our desperate need for Jesus, his love for us,
   and his sacrifice on the cross. We must often remember
   his resurrection and the power it provides to us. That
   he is sufficient for our every need. To apply his Holy
   Spirit's enablement in our daily lives. To appropriate his
   grace that is so abundantly available to us. And to daily
   recognize Jesus' divine right to rule in our lives. These
   are some of the things these Christians had once received
   and heard (1 Timothy 1:18-26; 2 Timothy 2:2; 1 John
   1:1-4).

4. "Keep it" (verse 3)—But what is "it"? Those things
   "you have received and heard." Paul put it this way to
   Timothy: "Guard what has been entrusted to you"
   (1 Timothy 6:20). Lay hold once again of the doctrinal
   foundation that got you started. Choose to re-embrace
   those truths.

5. "Repent" (verse 3)—Jesus wanted them to change their
   mind and choose to turn away from what they were
   trusting in and seeking.

Apparently, for those at Sardis, the process to fully wake this bride
and restore her to a right relationship to Jesus was one that involved
making several important decisions.

Jesus' Warning (3:3)

"If you do not [repent], I will come like a thief"—This refers to imminent, sudden judgment. Jesus said, "You will not know at what hour I will come." His visit would be a complete surprise to them. Put simply, Christ urges them to choose revival…or else.

Jesus' Promise (3:5)

What can "he who overcomes" expect from Christ? (verse 5).

- "I will not erase his name from the book of life."
- "I will confess his name before My father and before his angels."

In the Greco-Roman era, a person's name could be erased from the public record. John Chrysostom (a fourth-century early church father) described how citizens of Greek cities would lose their citizenship and have their names erased from specific roles if they were condemned for a criminal act. As we saw earlier, the phrase *damnatio memoriae* ("a condemnation of memory") describes this practice, and it was even applied to the Emperor Domitian because of his ultra-harsh tactics against people.

Among Christians, however, there has been some confusion regarding Christ's words here in Revelation 3:5. Some turn this comforting promise ("I will not erase") into a threat. But Jesus is not saying he will take someone's salvation away. That misses the point entirely, and the rest of Scripture flatly contradicts this possibility (John 10:27-29; 17:24; Romans 8:29-39; Hebrews 7:23-25). Instead, he is saying just the opposite: He will *never* take our salvation away. The residents of Sardis would have been familiar with the city's citizen registry. When someone died or committed a serious crime, their name was erased from the registry. Jesus is saying, "I will never ever do that to my own" (see Philippians 4:3; Revelation 13:8; 17:8; 20:12, 15; 21:27).

Contextually, Jesus is saying, "Don't worry. I will never do to you what those in your culture do to certain persons who have committed criminal or condemnable acts. I won't erase your name from my book like they do from theirs!"[2] John MacArthur has often said, in effect, "If it were possible for you to lose your salvation, trust me, you would."

Jesus is saying to those overcoming true believers that he would never erase their names because they have been written in the Lamb's book of life from before the foundation of the world—that is, eternity past (Daniel 12:1; Luke 10:20; Ephesians 1:4-5; Philippians 4:3; Revelation 3:5; 13:8; 20:15; 21:27). So we should read Jesus' words as a promise to the saved and not as a threat against them that they might lose their salvation.

To the contrary, Christ says he will confess those same overcomers before his Father, and before the angels, affirming to all of heaven that they belong to him (Matthew 10:32-33; Romans 8:28-39).

In Revelation 3:6, Jesus closes by saying, "He who has an ear, let him hear what the Spirit says to the churches." But did anyone at Sardis listen? What eventually happened to the church in that elevated, fortified city? Did the people ever repent? Did they wake up? Did they strengthen themselves as Jesus urged them to do?

History records that the church there did indeed continue for thirteen more centuries. So it appears that the people repented and followed the Lord's admonitions.

The most prominent member of the church at Sardis was a man by the name of Melito, who served as Bishop of Sardis in the late second century AD. He wrote the earliest known commentary on passages from the book of Revelation. So some type of revival was indeed ignited at Sardis, perhaps through this very letter and the book of Revelation itself!

The church at Sardis teaches us that we can never rest on past victories or achievements. Every day brings new challenges and reasons to trust God. We also learn that Christian activity is never a substitute for a personal relationship with Jesus. We must always seek to strengthen ourselves, keeping our hearts and spirits refreshed and recharged in his Word. And we can also be encouraged by the knowledge that churches can be reborn to new life!

Philadelphia—the Faithful Church (Revelation 3:7-13)

Philadelphia was the youngest of the seven cities in Revelation 2–3. It's the modern-day Turkish city of Alashir.[3] The ancient city was founded by the king of Pergamum, Attalus II (Philadelphus), who reigned from 159–138 BC. The Romans had tried to turn him against his brother (Eumenes II), but he remained loyal to him, thus earning the name *Philadelphia*, which means "brotherly love."

The city was an important stop on the imperial mail route and was home to ten gods and goddesses, as well as the imperial cult of Caesar. It was also located in a volcanic region that included fertile soil well suited for grapes (one of the city's principal crops).

In AD 17, the area suffered from a massive earthquake. And Philadelphia, being very near the epicenter, was devastated. Because of the frequent aftershocks, many of the residents relocated outside the city to live in huts, wanting to avoid the constant threat of a new disaster that could surprise them at any time. Not much remains of the city today.

Jesus' Revelation (3:7)

The Lord provides the Philadelphian disciples a fourfold description of himself.

1. He is "holy"—Primarily, this word means to be "set apart" (Greek *hagios*). The idea is that Jesus, being God, is different and unlike all others. He is unique and transcendent, self-existent and self-sufficient. Secondarily,

his holiness signifies that he is inherently without sin (1 Peter 1:15).

2. He is "true"—Jesus is the same "faithful witness" we saw in Revelation 1:5. This means he is consistent in his character and that he cannot lie (Titus 1:2). His truth is grounded in himself, and vice versa. All of God's attributes are interlinked and inseparable, and simultaneously true of him at all times. In the book of Revelation, he is often characterized by his holiness and truth (4:8; 6:10; 15:3; 16:7; 19:2, 4). Because he is true, he always speaks truth, and that includes the prophecies in Revelation.

3. He has "the key of David"—The last part of this verse is nearly a direct quote from Isaiah 22:22. As the prophesied Messiah and heir to David's throne, Jesus possesses the authority to determine who would be admitted into the future Davidic (millennial) kingdom (2 Samuel 7:16-17; Ezekiel 37:24; Hosea 3:5).

4. He opens doors "no one will shut"—In other words, he is sovereign and does as he pleases (Psalm 115:3). God can make a way where there is no way, creating divine opportunities for his chosen ones (Job 42:2). Conversely, he shuts doors "no one opens." His power cannot be denied or diminished. No king, president, premier, prime minister, antichrist, or fallen angel (Satan) can stop him from accomplishing his will (Daniel 4:35). This speaks to God's great sovereignty, which we will learn much more about it in the next chapter.

Jesus' Declaration (3:8)

Well aware of the Philadelphians' faithfulness, he who has the keys opens a door for them, likely an opportunity for gospel witness and ministry (see 1 Corinthians 16:9; 2 Corinthians 2:12; Colossians 4:3).

Jesus' Commendation (3:8, 10)

This church has "a little power." It's small, and not highly influential (see Luke 12:32; 1 Corinthians 1:26; 2 Corinthians 12:10). But the Philadelphian believers have also kept Christ's word and not denied his name. This speaks of their steadfast loyalty to him in the midst of a pagan culture (see 2 Thessalonians 3:5).

Jesus also mentions again the "synagogue of Satan" (Revelation 3:9), a probable allusion to unbelieving Jews who were causing trouble for local Christians. This highlights the principle that real ministry often invites opposition, many times from the religious crowd. According to Jesus, these are not true Jews, namely because they are fighting against the very plan and provision of the God of the old covenant (see Romans 2:28-29; 9:6-7). They were Jews physically, but not spiritually.

Jesus' prophecy to "make them come and bow down at your feet" either means that these Jews will be defeated and pay homage to these Philadelphian Gentile Christians (a complete reversal of what these Jews expected from Isaiah 60:14). Or that, in the millennial kingdom, ethnic Jews who have become believers in the Messiah will render homage to members of the body of Christ.

Jesus praises these believers, saying, "You have kept the word of My perseverance." They had hung in there during the worst of times. They didn't give up, give in, or give out. They exhibited one of the true marks of a believer—perseverance (Colossians 1:22-23).

Jesus' Rebuke

Christ has no correcting or disciplinary words for these faithful believers.

Jesus' Counsel (3:11)

The Lord advises them to "hold fast what you have." He tells them to keep being who they are, and keep believing, so that their heavenly reward is protected and that they will retain the crown that awaits them.

Jesus' Warning

There is no warning for the Philadelphian church.

Jesus' Promise (3:10, 12)

Jesus says, "I will also keep you from the hour of testing, that hour which is about to come upon the whole world, to test those who dwell on the earth." But what specifically does this promise mean?

Generally speaking, believers are not promised deliverance from testing or trials (James 1:2, 12; 1 Peter 1:6). But the key to understanding this statement is found in noting the contextual meaning of this particular "testing." So what can we learn upon taking a closer look at this verse?

1. The test is *future* ("about to come"). As of AD 95, when John is writing this, no such test had occurred on the earth. Further, if Revelation's AD 95 date is true, there is no credibility to what is called preterism, or the belief that Revelation's events have already taken place Preterism cannot be true because the events of Revelation 6–19 have yet to occur anywhere or at any time in history, and certainly did not take place during the first century and the destruction of Jerusalem in AD 70.

2. The test is *global* ("upon the whole world"). It's not a local or regional tribulation, but one that will impact the entire planet. Again, there has never been such a worldwide hour of testing.

3. The test is *targeted*, testing "those who dwell on the earth." This phrase is used 11 times throughout Revelation to specifically refer to unbelievers on the earth during the time of the seven-year tribulation (3:10; 6:10; 8:13; 11:10 [twice]; 13:8, 12, 14 [twice]; 14:6; 17:8), and always designates those who reject God. This tells us that one of the primary purposes of the tribulation is to bring retribution on the planet and to punish sinners with God's end-times wrath. Those who refuse to repent will fail the test (6:15-17; 9:20; 16:11; 19:17-18).

According to this verse, Jesus' bride is exempt from this global hour of testing (1 Thessalonians 1:10; 5:9). She will be delivered from the duration/hour/time of this season of judgment, which is also known as Daniel's 70th week (Daniel 9:25-27).

God's wrath during this period is not intended for those who have already been spared from judgment—that is, those who have received salvation in Christ.

Another thing to note here is John's specific word choice. In Revelation 3:10, Jesus uses the phrase *tereo ek*, which means to guard or keep "out of" or "away from" the "hour of testing." He could have used *en* or *dia*, meaning that he would keep us "in" or "through" the time of tribulation wrath. And God did preserve Daniel's friends Shadrach, Meshach, and Abednego while they were in a fiery furnace (Daniel 3). But those righteous men were facing man's wrath, not God's.

Tereo ek ("keep from") is more similar to how Lot's deliverance is described (*out of* Gomorrah), not Daniel's friends (*through* the fire).

These words are also used in John 17:15, where Jesus prays that his disciples will remain "out of" the dominion of the evil one, which, of course, we are (Colossians 1:13; 1 John 5:19-20).

This promise does not make sense if the rapture occurs at the end of the tribulation, for by that time, the church would have suffered through *all* of God's tribulation wrath. The problem with the "preservation through" view is that the Philadelphian church never went through the time of tribulation as described in Revelation 6–19. That's because it is still a future event.

Therefore, the hour of testing here can only be referring to the seven-year tribulation, as there has not been a divine judgment on earth, like that described in Revelation 6–19. Further evidence that Jesus was referring to the future tribulation is that this testing is specifically aimed at "those who dwell on the earth," not believers. As we have seen, this phrase is used throughout Revelation to describe those who actually do face the tribulation period (Revelation 17:12-14).

Additionally, Scripture is clear that those who come to faith during the tribulation won't be kept "from the hour of testing," but rather, brutally murdered (6:9-11; 7:9-14; 20:4).

Last, the church, the bride of Christ, is portrayed as being absent during the tribulation (see previous chapter on pages 40-42).

Next, Jesus tells the Philadelphian church, "I am coming quickly" (verse 11). In this context, his "coming" is not referring to the second coming, when he will judge his enemies (Revelation 19). Rather, this coming is one of deliverance.

The word "quickly" (Greek *taxy*) means "promptly, swiftly, without unnecessary delay." It doesn't convey the idea of "immediately" or in a "short time" chronologically, but rather, without delay (Revelation 22:7, 12, 20).

Jesus then gives, in Revelation 3:12, these promises to the Philadelphian believers:

- "He who overcomes, I will make him a pillar in the

temple of My God" (i.e., the New Jerusalem—Revelation chapters 21–22). Pillars were the main supports for temples in those days (the Temple of Serapis in Ephesus had 8 columns of 50 tons each). As pillars, we will be an important part of God's future dwelling.

- "He will not go out from it anymore." This means we will have permanent residence in this dwelling place. We will face no exposure to enemy threats. We'll live in an eternal place of honor, a place of citizenship. And unlike what the Philadelphians had experienced, there will be no earthquakes there!

- "I will write on him…the name of the city of My God." Columns in Ephesian temples had the names of civic, town, and cultural elites and officials engraved on them. This was a visible display of honor. As symbolic pillars in God's temple, we will enjoy being honored by him as well.

- "I will write on him the name of My God." In Scripture, a name designates character and association. In the New Jerusalem, we will be transformed and identified as belonging to God. A familial sign of intimacy and identification will be placed upon us.

All other churches, then and now, should pay close attention to what the Spirit is saying to the church at Philadelphia (Revelation 3:13).

Laodicea—the Lukewarm Church (3:14-22)

Laodicea was a part of the tri-cities (Colossae, Hierapolis, Laodicea). It had a large Jewish population (7,500 men). A wealthy city, it paid for its own reconstruction after the earthquake of AD 60. Laodicea was famous for soft, black, wool that was used for clothes and carpets.

It also boasted a medical school that exported an eye salve (called Phrygian powder) all over the Greco-Roman world. So the dominant industries in this city were wool and medicine. Paul mentions this church in Colossians 2:1; 4:15.

Jesus' Revelation (3:14)

Christ gives three key truths about who he is:

1. I am "the Amen." This title for Jesus is used only here (although in Isaiah 65:16, the Lord is called "the God of truth"). The Hebrew and Greek words are the same when transliterated—"amen," meaning "of a truth," "in support of" or "so let it be." This means Jesus is the truth, the affirmation, the certainty. He is firm, fixed, and unchangeable. In the New Testament, whenever the Lord says, "Truly, truly" (KJV) or "Verily, verily," it's this word that translates to "amen." Second Corinthians 1:20 says that "through Him is our *Amen* to the glory of God through us." Amen!

2. I am "the faithful and true Witness" (see John 1:14; 14:6; Revelation 1:5). He is the one who amplifies the amen. Everything he speaks is true, trustworthy, and reliable. He is even more reliable than we have believed or proved him to be!

3. I am "the Beginning of the creation of God." This doesn't mean Jesus was created first, but that he is the *source* (Greek *arche*) or *origin* of creation. In Colossae, there was a form of gnosticism that taught that Christ was a created being and an emanation from God. Paul addressed this in Colossians 1:15-17, stating that he is instead the source of creation and the preeminent "firstborn" (Greek *prototokos*) or supreme one.

Jesus' Declaration (3:15)

Jesus told the church at Laodicea, "I know your deeds." He is well aware of their spiritual condition and is about to lift the mask off this congregation.

Jesus' Commendation

The Lord has no praise or words of encouragement for them.

Jesus' Rebuke (3:15-17)

Jesus tells these people that they are "neither cold nor hot; I wish that you were cold or hot." Let's unpack the meaning of this statement by looking at some background information about the area.

Laodicea originally received its hot water from Hierapolis, which had hot springs, and its cooler water from Colossae, which had access to colder mountain water. However, by the time the waters reached the city, they were neither hot nor cold. This was, in part, due to the fact the water flowed for miles in underground aqueducts. But by the time it arrived it was dirty and tepid, and repulsive to drink.

Jesus taps into this distinctive about the city's water, telling the people they are just like that water. They are not hot, or passionate for him, nor are they cold, or apathetic to the gospel. Instead, they are in the middle, or lukewarm. They are content to be mediocre. Religious. Christianized. Satisfied. Settled. They think they are saved and that all is well (see Matthew 7:22-23; 2 Timothy 3:5).

Then Jesus lands the spiritual knockout punch: "So because you are lukewarm...I will spit you out of My mouth" (Revelation 3:16). The word "spit" (Greek *emeo*) means "to utterly reject with extreme disgust." To vomit.

This church makes Jesus sick, causing him to reject them in their current state. He refuses to accept them "as they are." It's as if he is saying, "You're not worthless to me, just *useless* to me. And because of your present condition, I cannot have a relationship with you."

Can you imagine Jesus Christ saying something like that to you? "I'm sorry, but I can't use you. You're *un*-usable. No good to me for the gospel's sake or for my kingdom." This is similar to what we read in Luke 14:34-35, where Jesus compares faux disciples to salt that has lost its flavor. It's good for *nothing*.

So what does it look like to be lukewarm?

- You don't act like you need Jesus.
- You live like Jesus is unimportant to you.
- You aren't really that desperate for Jesus.
- You can do church without Jesus.
- You think you're cool and self-sufficient.
- You love yourself more than you love Jesus.
- You have lost the gratitude you once had for your salvation.
- You are ignorant of reality and insensitive to the Holy Spirit.
- You have no clue as to how destitute, bankrupt, empty, blind, and naked you really are.
- Your condition is obvious to everyone but you.
- You neglect prayer and no longer have an attitude of dependence on the Lord.
- You can write your name in the dust on top of your Bible.
- You rely on your personality and natural talent, not the Holy Spirit.
- You are hard to convince of your problem because you think you're okay.

- You have no passion, and possess very little knowledge of the Lord.

- You trust your feelings instead of trusting in his Word and walking by faith.

Next, Jesus exposes the heart attitudes of those in the church at Laodicea: "You say, I am rich...and have need of nothing." The Laodiceans have a false sense of security and salvation. But Christ tells them they are not rich, but rather, "wretched and miserable and poor and blind and naked" (Revelation 3:17).

Jesus' Counsel (3:18)

In his prescription for curing lukewarmness, Jesus alludes to the city's three points of pride (wealth, fabric, medicine).

He tells them, to buy from him *true redemption*:

- "Buy from Me gold refined by fire so that you might become rich." He says, "What I give has no impurities. They are true riches, and better than what you have." He wanted them to rearrange their priorities and find the riches of life found in him alone, and not in material goods.

- "Buy from Me...white garments so that you may clothe yourself, and that the shame of your nakedness will not be revealed." These white garments picture salvation and righteousness, an imagery repeated throughout Revelation (3:4-5; 4:4; 6:11; 7:9, 13-14; 19:8).

- "Buy from Me...eye salve to anoint your eyes so that you may see." Blinded and dulled by their pride and mediocrity, their lack of spiritual sight and understanding kept them from the life Jesus offered (see Acts 26:18).

Jesus tells them, in essence, "You must get these things from me because you have nothing to offer me" (see Isaiah 64:5-6; Ephesians 2:1-3). This is their only salvation from the lukewarmness that threatened to steal their soul. And so Christ graciously offers them a second chance and a way out of their mediocrity.

And yet, even in his rebuke, he wants them to know he still loved them. "Those whom I love [Greek *phileo*], I reprove [Revelation 3:19; John 16:18] and "discipline" (in 2 Timothy 2:25, where the word refers to training up a child). Jesus doesn't reprove or discipline the unsaved, only his children (Hebrews 12:5-11). The fact that he is rebuking the church in Laodicea is a sure sign of his enduring love for these believers.

Jesus' Warning (3:16, 19)

So what is needed from these people? What does the Lord require from mediocre, lukewarm Christians?

In a word, repentance. Corporate, zealous repentance. He urges them to be passionate and intentional about turning from their complacency and back to him (see Acts 11:18; 1 Thessalonians 1:9). Unless they repent, Jesus will reject them as a church, and they will have zero effectiveness for him (see Revelation 2:5).

Jesus' Promise (3:20-21)

Christ then says he is knocking on the door of the church (verse 20). It's ironic that he is outside his own church, the one bearing his name. The one he himself founded. The one he promised to build. The one for whom he suffered and died. Jesus wants back inside his church. He wants to be invited inside the church and have a close relationship with the people again, and repentance is the key that unlocks the church door. If just one person opens that door, Jesus will enter the church through that person and begin to "dine with him, and he with Me" (verse 20). The word "dine" here refers to the evening meal—the last meal of the day—and pictures fellowship, closeness, and intimacy.

The Bible says that one day we will dine at the marriage supper of the Lamb (Revelation 19:9) as well as during the millennial kingdom (Luke 22:16, 29-30), but Jesus also wants to spiritually and relationally dine with us *now*—individually, and corporately with his churches.

And what will happen if the Laodicean believers overcome this crippling disease of lukewarmness? Jesus promised to honor them by letting them sit with him on his throne (Revelation 3:21). They will co-reign with Christ as he elevates their status in his future kingdom.

Those Who Overcome

What we have discovered so far is that all those in the church who are overcomers will gain the following—they will...

- eat from the tree of life (2:7)
- receive the crown of life (2:10)
- be protected from the second death (2:11)
- receive hidden manna (2:17)
- receive a white stone with a new name written on it (2:17)
- receive authority to rule the nations (2:26-27)
- receive the morning star (2:28)
- be clothed in white garments (3:5)
- hear Christ confess them before the Father (3:5)
- be made a pillar in God's temple (3:12)
- have God's name written on them (3:12)

Now *there's* motivation to persevere to the end and be an overcomer!

Finally, in Revelation 3:22, Jesus closes with these words: "He who has an ear, let him hear what the Spirit says to the churches."

We've now surveyed the seven churches Jesus chose to address in his last-ever written book. Far from merely being past historical examples to us (which they are), these congregations serve as a lasting reminder of the dangers of doctrinal deviance and spiritual mediocrity. Yes, it matters very much what churches believe and teach. And it matters how the people live. Why? Because Jesus is watching every one of them—evaluating, discerning, and preparing to either rebuke, reward, or regurgitate them.

What would Jesus say to the more than 300,000 churches in America today, at a time when we are experiencing the lowest levels of church attendance in our nation's history? What would his commendation be? Who would he rebuke, and why? I think we know some of the answers already. What would his counsel be? And what would he promise? Though there may be some additional words for today's churches, I strongly suspect that we would find him repeating the same words he spoke to the seven churches in Revelation 2–3. We read their stories and see in them a mirror image of the church today. Some have lost their first love. Some are enduring persecution. Others are doctrinally sound yet cold. Some are doctrinally deviant. Some are filled with worldly values. Some embrace immorality. Some are lukewarm. And some are dead.

If we take anything away from the examples set by these seven churches, apart from their sins, sufferings, and seeking of Christ, let's not forget that our Lord loves his bride and has bound himself to keep building her, refining her, purifying her, and preparing her for the day he returns to rescue her from the time of wrath that is coming upon this world.

A TRIP TO THE THRONE ROOM

The God Who Is *Sovereign*

Revelation 4:1-11

N ow that Jesus has shown John the condition of the churches on Earth, it's time for the aged apostle to learn what things are like in heaven. John looks to see a door standing open in heaven. This open door represents an invitation to enter, which is confirmed by a heavenly trumpet voice (likely the same voice he heard back in Revelation 1:10 which was the voice of Jesus Christ). This speaker invites John, "*Come up here*, and I will show you what must take place after these things" (Revelation 4:1).

It's worth noting that "Come up here" are the exact words the two witnesses will hear after they are murdered by the antichrist and brought back from the dead by God (Revelation 11:12). In both cases, the hearers were suddenly summoned up to heaven. And though the two witnesses will ascend physically, John traveled to heaven spiritually, in a vision. Some have wondered if these could be the same words heard by the bride of Christ at Jesus' rapture appearing (1 Thessalonians 4:16). Other commentators also see John's visit to heaven as a symbolic foreshadow of the rapture itself. And as will happen with the blessed hope, or the rapture, John seems to have little choice in the matter, for Jesus' authoritative command is irresistibly obeyed.

The reason Jesus gives this invitation is so that he can show John the rest of Revelation's prophecies. And apparently the travel time wasn't long, as John was "immediately...in the Spirit" (Revelation 4:2). This experience of being "in the Spirit" seems to be a continuation of the vision he had originally received in Revelation 1:10. However, the geography of the vision experience in chapters 1–3 was different. There, Jesus came to John. But now in chapter 4, John comes to Jesus, placing him in the very near presence of the Father.

God's Heavenly Throne

Once John finds himself in heaven, what first captivates him is not the angels nor the number of saints already there. No, what arrests his attention is something far more grandiose, ominous, and impressive. It's a throne and him who sat upon it. John is about to receive a God-sized glimpse of how things work in heaven—a vision of the royal, regal government of the galaxies. The apostle's eyes become riveted on the centerpiece of heaven.

So prominent is this throne that John mentions it 13 times in 11 verses. Repetition is one of the primary ways John emphasizes some of the more important truths in Revelation. And here, what John discovers about the heavenly throne will prove to be a major game changer not only for the remainder of Revelation, but also for the rest of our lives. From John's eyewitness account we learn several truths about this throne:

The Throne Is Occupied (4:2)

This throne is described as "standing," meaning it is "established from eternity, unmovable, permanent." The throne is set in stone, if you will. And the reason is because God is seated there, and this is his eternal throne. It is from this position that royalty rules. It's where the king of all the universe resides. He is the creator, the eternal one—God almighty.

The Bible tells us God's rule is established, and that from his throne eternal decrees are issued (Isaiah 14:26-27; 46:9-10; Daniel 4:35). Among these decrees are

- the stability of the universe (Psalm 119:89-91),
- the times and boundaries of nations (Acts 17:26), and
- the length of human life (Job 14:1, 5).

From the throne also comes the sovereign choice of a people for God's own possession (John 6:44; Romans 9–11; Ephesians 1:1). And finally, this throne issues forth the divine judgments we see unfolding throughout the tribulation (Revelation 6:16).

The Throne Is Beautiful (4:3)

Using the language of his day, John does his best to describe the one he sees sitting on the throne. Here, God has the appearance of jasper and sardius. Jasper has a crystal-clear, diamond-like appearance (cf. Revelation 21:11, where the new Jerusalem also reflects this brilliant glory of God).

Sardius is a ruby-colored stone. John MacArthur writes that these two stones "were the first and last stones on the high priest's breastplate (Exodus 28:17-20; ruby, jasper), representing the firstborn (Reuben) and last born (Benjamin) of the 12 sons of Jacob."[1]

However, the exact meaning or symbolism of these brilliant-colored jewels is not given. Rather than speculate, let's just let them speak for themselves. John sees God as one who emanates brilliance, beauty, and glory.

John continues, telling us that around the throne is a "rainbow... like an emerald in appearance" (Revelation 4:3). Notice throughout Revelation John's frequent use of the word "like," signifying that he's trying to describe what he *sees* as compared to describing what he already *knows* about. To accomplish this, he employs the literary device "like" as a means of conveying that what he's looking at is indescribable. This clearly reveals how limited our language is when it comes to describing our indescribable God. Words, and even word pictures, fall short. We must therefore resign ourselves to being content with descriptive terms that cannot adequately capture what John is actually seeing.

Suffice it to say that the glorious colors of heaven are beyond what human eyes have ever seen, and that the God who rules there is far greater than mortal minds can comprehend.

The Throne Is Revered (4:4)

Surrounding this throne John sees 24 thrones, upon which are 24 "elders." But who are these elders? And why are there 24 of them? We know they cannot be angels, because nowhere in Scripture do angels sit on thrones or receive heavenly crowns. The most plausible explanation is that they are representatives of the redeemed bride of Christ. This is the preferred interpretation, for four reasons:

1. They're clothed in white garments. Jesus offered the churches at Sardis and Laodicea white garments (Revelation 3:5, 18). In Revelation 19:8, we also see the church in heaven clothed in fine linen, bright and clean, and she will return with Christ at his second coming wearing these same garments (verse 14). While it's true that angels also wear similar white linen in Revelation

15:6 and accompany Jesus and us at the second coming (Matthew 25:31; Jude 1:14), it's here where the similarities end.

2. They are wearing golden crowns. These crowns (Greek *stephanos*) are awarded to those in the church who endure and live for Christ while on earth (1 Corinthians 9:25; 2 Timothy 4:8; James 1:12; 1 Peter 5:4). Again, holy angels do not struggle with temptation nor earn heavenly rewards.

3. They occupy thrones, which indicates they are reigning with God. Angels minister for God, but they do not co-reign with him (Hebrews 1:14). By contrast, the church, the bride of Christ, is repeatedly described and pictured as reigning with Jesus (Revelation 2:26-27; 3:21; 5:10; 20:4; see also Matthew 19:28; Luke 22:30; 1 Corinthians 6:2-3; 2 Timothy 2:12).

4. Angels are never called "elders" in Scripture (Greek *presbuteros*). But the term does apply to those within the church (Acts 20:27; 24:23; 1 Timothy 3:5; 1 Peter 5:2).

So what is the significance of the number 24 here? Some have suggested that it represents Israel and the church—12 tribes and 12 apostles. And though the math certainly works out, the theology doesn't. Old Testament saints will not be rewarded until after the tribulation (Daniel 12:1-3). The 24 also cannot represent the tribulation saints because at this point, they have yet to be redeemed. So, if the evidence points to this number representing the church or bride of Christ, the only question remaining is this: Why 24?

We do see this number used to represent completion or wholeness in the Bible (1 Chronicles 24:4-5, 7-18; 25). We also see that David divided the tribe of Levi into 24 parts, representing the whole number of priests. So without any other compelling biblical reason to interpret the number otherwise, it seems to make sense that these 24 elders signify a complete representation of the greater body of Christ, the church. We see these elders mentioned elsewhere throughout Revelation (11:15-18; 14:1-3; 19:1-4).

The Throne Is Righteous (4:5)

John sees coming from the throne "flashes of lightning and sounds and peals of thunder," which reverberate throughout heaven. Thunder appears repeatedly in the book of Revelation (6:1; 8:5; 11:19; 14:2; 16:18; 19:6) and represents the ominous, mighty, righteous, and wrathful works of God in judgment. Thunder is authoritative and intimidating. And here it could foreshadow God's righteous fury about to be displayed on earth. And John's audiovisual experience has just begun!

Next, John sees "seven lamps of fire" burning before the throne. These are immediately explained to be "the seven Spirits of God." The obvious question is, What does this phrase refer to? We've seen these same words before, back in Revelation 1:4. There, the "Seven spirits" seem to refer to the Holy Spirit himself, being mentioned in the same sentence along with the Father and the Son. But it could also be picturing the sevenfold ministry of the Spirit, which is described in Isaiah 11:2. The seven lamps may also have some allusion to the Jewish menorah, which is also a symbol of the Holy Spirit. Seven is the number of perfection, and could portray the Holy Spirit in all his fullness.

So, the seven lamps of fire are "the seven Spirits of God," which as we saw earlier represent the Holy Spirit in his completeness and perfection. We see the number 7 used 54 times in Revelation.

The Throne Is Holy (4:6-11)

In front of heaven's throne is "something like a crystal sea of glass" (Revelation 4:6).

We know from Revelation 21:1 that there is no actual sea in heaven. However, this crystal-like "sea of glass" before the throne is vast enough to resemble a body of water. Several other objects are compared to glass in Revelation, including the walls of the new Jerusalem (verse 18) and the golden streets of that city (verse 21). Those believers who won victory over antichrist by refusing the mark of the beast are standing on the sea of glass in Revelation 15:2.

In the middle of the throne, and around it, John is confronted by a bizarre sight. He sees "four living creatures," which he describes as being "full of eyes in front and behind" (Revelation 4:6). Though his description varies slightly from Ezekiel's, these are no doubt the same class of angel the Old Testament prophet saw. There, they're called "cherubim" (Ezekiel 10).

So these creatures are angels, and most likely of the cherubim class. But what do we know about them? The Bible tells us it was the cherubim who guarded the way to the tree of life after Adam and Eve sinned (Genesis 3:24). They are also represented in gold on the mercy seat of the ark of the covenant (Exodus 25:18-22).

And here in Revelation 4, we get a fuller description of them. Verse 6 says that are "full of eyes in front and behind." This likely pictures their knowledge and constant awareness. Though not omniscient like God, their ability to see and know is unparalleled among the other heavenly beings.

Then in verse 7, John describes the four creatures as follows: One is like a lion, which may speak of majesty and strength; one is like a calf, possibly representing humble service; one has "a face like that of a man," which may refer to intelligence or rational thought; and one is like a flying eagle, which may illustrate great vision and speedy service in carrying out a mission. In Ezekiel 1:10, the four cherubim possess all four characteristics.

In verse 8, John describes the cherubim's wings, and there are six of them Isaiah's seraphim class of angels also have six wings, which serve in this way: two to cover their face, two to cover their feet, and two for flying (Isaiah 6:2). However, the cherubim angels in Ezekiel only have four wings (1:6), leading some scholars to conclude that these four living creatures of Revelation are some sort of hybrid between the two, or even some other class of angel altogether.

By the way, according to Ezekiel, angels appear to travel at extreme speeds, their velocity being compared to that of lightning (Ezekiel 1:14).

And what are these cherubim doing? John sees and hears them incessantly proclaiming a core truth about the God they serve (Isaiah 6:3). And their refrain rings throughout the throne chamber "day and night," without pause. It's a chorus of praise announcing God's holiness: "Holy, holy, holy is the Lord God, the Almighty, who was and who is and who is to come" (Revelation 4:8).

Why do they repeat "holy"? Why this attribute? Why not "love"? Or "good"? Or "awesome"? Or "faithful"?

The answer lies in the fact that these angels know something about God that we don't. Because of their exposure and proximity to him, along with their enhanced ability to comprehend truth, these cherubim understand something of God's *essence*, something concerning his core nature that is rarely talked about today in churches and Bible studies.

The four angels do not primarily praise God for what he has done, but rather, for *who he is*. Sadly, in our consumer Christian culture, we can easily fall into the trap of thinking (and acting) as if God exists for our benefit. This is taken to the extreme in the aberrant Word of Faith movement, which promotes a dangerous heresy that believes Christians have become "little gods" through their "faith-driven ability" to conjure up self-blessings at will, perform healings, and produce prosperity and good fortune by merely speaking it into reality. But this is not the theology of heaven at all. Around the throne, privileged angels are obsessed with God and God alone. These are what I call "elevator thoughts"—they elevate our thinking toward heaven, causing us to think lofty thoughts about our Lord. This is how we can "go deep" with God—by allowing the truths of heaven to influence our minds and hearts here on earth.

So in what sense is holiness a core attribute of God?

The word translated "holy" primarily means "to be separate, set apart." In Hebrew, the word is *qadosh*, meaning "to set apart," or "to separate." In Greek, it's *hagios*—"to be different, unlike, set apart," and as it relates to God, "highly exalted."

Therefore, to declare God as holy means he is incomparable, unequaled, and unlike any human, angel, or created being. It speaks of his transcendence, or the fact that he is so inexpressibly above us as to be incomprehensible. Theologians sometimes refer to God as being "wholly other." In other words, his essence exists on a plane far above human comprehension or experience. Trying to wrap your mind around this truth would be like trying to capture the entire universe in one photograph. It simply can't be done.

God's inherent holiness is one of his incommunicable attributes. In other words, we can never know it or experience it ourselves.

Even in our future glorified state, we will never be transcendent like him. The prophet Isaiah pictures this reality as it relates to God's mind and deeds, writing,

> "My thoughts are not your thoughts,
>   nor are your ways My ways," declares the LORD.
> "For as the heavens are higher than the earth,
>   so are My ways higher than your ways,
>   and My thoughts than your thoughts"
>   (Isaiah 55:8-9).

And just how high are the heavens above the earth? There are billions, even trillions of stars and galaxies, separated by millions of light-years in every direction. Try and grasp this with your mind for 60 seconds, or even 6 seconds. Stand on your intellectual and philosophical tiptoes and attempt to grasp a small fraction of this truth. Think of the immeasurable physical distance between you here on earth and some faraway, remote star or planet. We simply are not mentally equipped to go there. It's like trying to fit the Pacific Ocean into a thimble.

This is what it's like for you and me to try to fully understand the essential holiness of God. Furthermore, holiness is actually the sum total of all God's attributes. His grace is holy. His love is holy. His justice is holy. His mercy is holy. His sovereignty is holy. His righteousness is holy. He is holy. This concept is largely foreign to the average Christian today. But when contemplated, it leads us all to one grand conclusion: This God, who is seated on heaven's throne, is not like us.

Not at all.

But as believers, we can, and do, experience the secondary aspect of his holiness—that of being righteous and free from the domain of sin and its dominance. This is the gift we received from him at the moment of our salvation. It is a holiness and righteousness that is imputed to us upon placing faith in Jesus. Sometimes referred to as "the great exchange," God the Father placed our sin and his eternal wrath on the Son while the Son hung on the cross. Second Corinthians 5:21 clearly states that God "made Him who knew no sin to be sin on our behalf." The Father treated Christ the same way he will treat sinners one day—totally abandoning them while simultaneously blasting them with eternal, fierce wrath (Revelation 14:10-11).

That is what happened at the cross: an eternity's worth of righteous fury and anger against sin was supernaturally compressed into six hours' time. At the cross, our Savior paid our sin debt in full. This is why, after his suffering was complete, Jesus cried out, "It is finished!" (John 19:30). The Greek word here is *tetelestai*, which technically means "to fulfill one's task or mission." This was Jesus' cry of "Mission accomplished!" But the verb was also used in secular Greek culture to refer to a tax debt being paid.

Because of Jesus, we who have trusted in him no longer owe any-thing on our sin debt to God. But even better is the second half of 2 Corinthians 5:21, which states this was done "that we might become the righteousness of God in Him." So Jesus took our sin. And we received his righteousness. *His* righteousness. Not ours made better, because we never had any to begin with (Romans 3:10-12, 23). As a result, we are now clothed with the very holy condition of God him-self! And that is the only reason we are allowed into heaven.

Would you pause and reflect for a moment on this glorious and wonderful truth? We who were once depraved (Jeremiah 17:9), unrigh-teous (Romans 5:6-8), dead in sin (Ephesians 2:2), separated from the life of God (Isaiah 59:2; Ephesians 2:12) and condemned to a Christ-less eternity in hell (John 3:18, 36; Romans 6:23) have now, by his grace, been saved (Romans 5:10), forgiven (Ephesians 1:7), adopted (Ephesians 1:5), brought near (Ephesians 2:13), made alive (Ephe-sians 2:4), made righteous (2 Corinthians 5:21), and given hope and an eternal home in heaven (John 14:1-3; Ephesians 2:6-9).

How does that make you feel? And how do you respond to such lavish love, grace, and mercy from a thrice-holy God?

A Proper Response to God

There is only one appropriate response to this truth, other than utter humility, and that's grateful worship. In Revelation 4:9-11, we see one of 14 doxologies (songs of praise) in Revelation. If you have ever needed to jump-start your mind and heart into a spirit of wor-ship on a Sunday morning, this is how to do it. You want to wor-ship, but your mind is wandering and your heart is hesitant. That's part of our human frailty. It's difficult to push ourselves to "worship on demand." But in heaven, there is no such struggle.

Prompted by the four living creatures, the 24 elders (who repre-sent the bride of Christ) burst into a chorus of adoration, giving their "amen" in response to the angelic proclamations of God's character.

Falling down before the Lord and casting their crowns at his feet, they cry out, "Worthy are You, our Lord and our God, to receive glory and honor and power; for You created all things, and because of Your will they existed, and were created" (4:11).

Notice that in heaven, God is still worshipped for being the creator of all things.

But we not only worship him because he is the creator, but also because he is the *reason* for creation itself—it simply pleased him to create. Paul wrote concerning Christ, "All things have been created *through* Him and *for* Him" (Colossians 1:16). He is not only the cause of creation and the instrument of it, but also the goal of it as well. We exist for him. The point of our existence *is* God.

But this wasn't the only time the apostle found himself lost in the greatness of God's transcendence and sovereignty. To the Romans, he declared,

> Oh, the depth of the riches both of the wisdom and knowledge of God! How unsearchable are His judgments and unfathomable His ways! For who has known the mind of the Lord, or who became His counselor? Or who has first given to Him that it might be paid back to him again? For from Him and through Him and to Him are all things. To Him be the glory forever. Amen (Romans 11:33-36).

So why does Jesus show John, and us, this scene? Why follow up his evaluation of the churches with a virtual trip to heaven? Here are four compelling reasons:

1. So we can know more of who our God really is. Beyond our vain and limited imaginations of what we think or hope he is, here we see him as the angels do. Of all the supposed "I died and went to heaven for thirty minutes" claims there are circulating in the church today, none

of them come close to describing heaven as John does in Revelation 4. That's because John saw the real heaven, not a version manufactured by human invention, mental trauma, or a dream.

2. So we can have a distinct advantage while living down here on earth. In heaven, all eyes are on the throne and him who occupies it. No one there is focused on their own needs or wants because God himself is the fulfillment of all we desire. I wonder how our present problems and struggles could be put into perspective if our eyes were on the throne more?

3. To demonstrate that our future is full of wonder, hope, joy, worship, and God.

4. To retroactively apply that future to our lives right now, giving us comfort, peace, rest, and security in the midst of a planet filled with chaos and sin.

Notice also the timing of this heavenly visit. When is John taken up to heaven? It's not during the tribulation that he discovers the elders (church) already there, but rather, *before* Revelation 6, when the seven-year tribulation officially begins. Perhaps Jesus wanted John, and us, to know that we (as represented by the 24 elders) would *already* be in heaven prior to the unleashing of his judgments on the earth. This idea fits the pre-tribulational rapture view best.

Therefore, we do not panic. We do not despair. We do not collapse. And we do not give in or give up.

Why not? One reason: There is a throne in heaven.

All is well there. God is in charge. There is no anxiety—only awe. Trials and tribulations are temporary. But the throne is forever.

How, then, can we not cope? How, then, can we not conquer? How, then, can we not worship?

Chapter 6

THE LION, THE LAMB, AND THE LITTLE BOOK

The God Who Is *Worthy*

Revelation 5:1-14

I f you're a golfer, it's Tiger Woods. To hockey fans, it's Wayne Gretzky. For baseball, Lou Gehrig or Babe Ruth. Basketball? Gotta be Michael Jordan. Art? Rembrandt. Rock group? Hands down, the Beatles. Boxing? Muhammad Ali. And the list could go on and on.

All these names are well-known to the world. And they are all known as the "GOAT," or Greatest of All Time. But why? Why are they considered the best? Because of their contributions to their respective fields? Yes, that's part of it. But dig a little deeper, and you'll discover that it was their overall *value* to their craft, sport, or field— and to a certain degree, to humanity itself. Those great ones did what almost no one had ever done before. What they accomplished is the reason why the world unanimously recognizes their right to that unique title, GOAT. And this prompts billions to say, "There'll never be another _____."

However, in heaven, golf's greatest player pales into insignificance. History's most storied athletes and most accomplished artists suddenly find their accomplishments and legacies to be irrelevant compared to what is found in heaven. All their achievements combined—records, points, home runs, number one hits, and masterpieces of art—all of them dissolve into nothingness when this life is over. What they did will not last forever.

As the story of mankind winds down and Bible prophecy ramps up to a climactic conclusion, heaven pauses to ponder the *real* hero of the ages. Already foreshadowed in the previous chapter, Revelation turns the page to show us yet another dramatic scene.

Journeying through the apocalypse, we discover there are two narratives being played out—one on earth, and the other in heaven. John sees him who occupies the celestial throne, a fitting portrayal of the holy one who lives and reigns forever and ever. Now his eyes are diverted to the *hand* of him who sits on that throne. In it he holds a book, or more properly, a rolled-up scroll. The word here is *biblion*, rendered "little scroll." This scroll is rolled up from the ends (cf. Revelation 6:14) and contains writing both on the inside and on the back.

It was an ancient Roman custom to seal wills, rental and lease agreements, bills and bonds, and other legal documents. In Jeremiah 32, we read of a Hebrew document that most resembles the kind described here in Revelation 5. And the document here in Revelation 5 is a scroll of doom—one containing judgment, but also redemption.[1]

As Revelation unfolds, we discover it to be a book that talks about judgments, kingdoms, and crowns. Essentially this little scroll unveils the culmination of redemption's story and the reconciliation of all things to God. And whoever is qualified to break the seals and open the scroll will be the one to whom the kingdoms of the earth will rightly belong.

The Title Deed

That brings us to this important question: Who rightfully owns the earth? Is it Satan, who currently dominates as "the prince of the power of the air"? (Ephesians 2:2). After all, Jesus himself called the devil "the ruler of this world" (John 12:31). Paul wrote that he is the "god of this world" (2 Corinthians 4:4). Earth is his domain and the realm of his kingdom (Colossians 1:13). And it is a deep-rooted reign, too, for the devil has ruled the kingdoms of this world since the early chapters of human history, when Satan first attempted to bring the world together under a single leader (Genesis 11). It is these earthly kingdoms that Satan offered to Jesus during the Lord's wilderness temptation (Matthew 4:8-10). And they legitimately were his to give (Luke 4:6-8). But Christ refused the ogre's offer, knowing that worshipping Satan (were it even possible for him to do) would disqualify him as our sinless substitute.

Or does the world belong to the antichrist? And is it in his destiny to own the title deed? Or does the planet belong to God, who originally granted co-regency to Adam, who, in turn, forfeited it through sin? Is Jesus now reclaiming that right for himself…and for us? We're about to find out, as next, a strong angel proclaims with a loud voice, "Who is worthy to open the book and to break its seals?" (Revelation 5:2).

As we've noted, whoever is worthy to do this is the one to whom the earth owes its worship. However, there must have been a pregnant pause in this scene as a search ensues and no one is found worthy—in heaven, or on the earth, or under the earth (the dead from past history). Among the living and the dead, the hunt continues. But heaven and earth come up empty. Upon this realization, John is overcome with emotion and begins to "weep greatly" (verse 4).

His cascade of emotions is understandable, both for him personally and for the future of redemption's story. He weeps because, from his perspective, the Messiah, following his death and resurrection, had ascended back to heaven. Since then, "the way" (as Christianity came to be known) had been marginalized, and its followers ridiculed and persecuted.

Then in AD 70, Jerusalem was attacked and its temple destroyed, just as Jesus had prophesied in Matthew 24:1-2. So as the first century AD raced toward the second, John witnessed...

- believers persecuted and martyred
- Jerusalem invaded
- the temple destroyed
- the Jewish people massacred
- the church compromised
- the world under the iron fist of Rome

John himself was arrested and exiled to a lonely, barren island. It would seem that he had every reason to be filled with despair. What he didn't know—and could not have—was that following the siege on his beloved Jerusalem in AD 70, the Jews would be scattered to the nations for some 1,900 years! But if this heavenly scroll isn't opened, earth will presumably remain under Satan's control in perpetuity. This means there will be no vindication for martyred believers and no redemption for Israel. God's prophetic Word will not be fulfilled. His plans will be thwarted. His kingdom will not come. In short, evil will win. Had John not been given this Revelation vision, his last written work may have more aptly been titled "Satan Is Alive and Well on Planet Earth!"

Glory Days of the Godless

No doubt, you have experienced similar emotions as you've

watched our country, and indeed, our entire world, continue its slide into delusional depravity. Evil governments and global elites rise to power, and presidents and prime ministers rule from thrones making decisions of which the devil himself would be proud. Mandates are declared, curtailing freedoms and destroying economies. Laws are passed that praise, celebrate, and protect sins that once prompted worldwide destruction and the wrath of God. And with Jeremiah, we cry out, "Why has the way of the wicked prospered? Why are those who deal in treachery at ease?" (Jeremiah 12:1-2). A similar sentiment is echoed in Job 21:7: "Why do the wicked still live, continue on, also become very powerful?"

The psalmist joins this chorus of lament:

> I was envious of the arrogant
> as I saw the prosperity of the wicked.
> For there are no pains in their death,
> and their body is fat (Psalm 73:2-4).

The writer honestly wonders if it's even worth continuing on the path of righteousness, saying, "Surely in vain have I kept my heart pure and washed my hands in innocence" (verse 13).

There was a time in our own country when, like dual watchmen, both the government and the culture "had our backs." Basic Judeo-Christian values, though not always practiced, were nevertheless upheld as the gold standard of morality, decency, and conduct. Marriage between a man and woman was civilization's norm for all of human history. Homosexuality and lesbianism were viewed as deviant, immoral, and against nature itself. Society and medicine rightly recognized only two genders. Governments and schools acknowledged God. Science universally attested that mankind was created by God. We didn't celebrate sin in the streets and designate an entire month of the year to revel in unapologetic "pride" over it. The majority of Americans went to church on Sundays. And we didn't brutally slaughter millions of innocent unborn babies without batting an eye. But all that has changed. The tide has turned. Morals have been redefined. Values reinterpreted. We are through the looking glass now. We are living in a surreal state. Laws now require the recognition of evil, protecting the depraved and deviant. *Love* is redefined as whatever you feel or want it to be. Truth is a personal construct, not an absolute, objective measure.

God is no longer the creator, if he even exists at all. All religions lead to "heaven," if there is such a place. Mankind exists for the pleasure and sustainability of the planet. We must now serve Mother Earth and bow to the fictitious god of "climate change."

Feelings overrule facts.

What was once profane is now sacred.

Evil is good. Good is evil.

Self is God.

Rogue institutions aggressively push a "global reset," unleashing a "fourth industrial revolution" where digital technology is being merged with the human body and mind. The same entities lobby for the replacement of Judeo-Christian values with self-worship and the blending of all faiths into one.

Religious attendance is at its lowest in nearly 100 years.[2]

The number of Americans identifying as something other than heterosexual has doubled since 2012.[3]

"Men" can now magically become "women" simply by imagining they are, even claiming to be able to have babies.

One can jump back and forth between genders, depending on how they "feel."

Children and teenagers now imagine themselves to be animals, becoming "furries" and being applauded by their peers and others at their schools.

It's clear that, as believers in Jesus, we no longer have the home-field advantage. Our tents are clearly pitched in the enemy's camp. Much like those in the early church and John himself, we are being marginalized, demonized, and canceled. And if Satan could have his way, we would be exterminated from the planet.

When All Hope Seemed Lost

We are living in a strange moment. A time of perilous change in which we're witnessing the emergence of a new dark age. And there's every indication the times will grow darker. So we ask, "Why?" and, "Is there any hope?"

Your brother John felt that despair too. To the point of tears. His soul was in anguish, even in heaven.

And to think it all comes down to one little scroll, a document representing the title deed to planet Earth, and the future of everything there is.

So, now perhaps we can empathize more fully with why the elderly apostle was weeping so bitterly.

But wait. As it turns out, John's tears are premature. And unnecessary. Like the tears shed by the widow at Nain and those who mourned over the synagogue ruler's daughter (Luke 7:13; 8:52). As we say in the South, the story "ain't over yet."

One of the 24 elders, whom we earlier identified as being symbolic representatives of the church, tells John to stop weeping. "Behold, the Lion that is from the tribe of Judah, the Root of David, has overcome so as to open the book and its seven seals" (Revelation 5:5).

"The Root of David" is a messianic title (Isaiah 11:1). Both Matthew 1 and Luke 3 reveal Jesus as a descendant of David on both his parents' sides (cf. Romans 1:3). And one reason he is qualified to take the book and open its seals is because he has "overcome." John uses the Greek word *nikao* here, meaning "to conquer, win, or be victorious" (see also Revelation 3:21). We get our English *nike* from this term. The original grammatical construction here has the verb at the beginning of the sentence, so it literally reads, "Behold, he has conquered, the lion that is from the tribe of Judah."

But what specifically has he overcome? According to Scripture...

1. sin (Romans 8:3)

2. death (Hebrews 2:14-15)

3. the forces of hell (Colossians 2:15; 1 Peter 3:19)

Jesus' victory at the cross, along with the empty tomb, earned him the right to take the scroll and break its seven seals. And the good news is that we can also overcome through him (Colossians 2:13-14; 1 John 5:5, Revelation 2:7, 1, 17, 26; 3:5, 12, 21).

At this point, John looks at the Lamb himself (Revelation 5:6). This is the most captivating sight in heaven. John first sees him as a lion (verse 5), and then a lamb (verse 6). The word for "lamb" here is *arnion*, a diminutive form of *arnos*, meaning "little lamb," or pet lamb (Exodus 12:3-6). Jesus is referred to as the Lamb only 4 times in the first 26 books of the New Testament (John 1:29, 36; Acts 8:32; 1 Peter 1:19). But in Revelation, he is called the Lamb 31 times!

Christ as the Lamb represents his first coming and refers to the Jewish Passover, when he would be sacrificed for our sins (John 1:29; 1 John 2:2). And Christ as the Lion refers to his second coming. This is the only place in the book of Revelation where Jesus is referred to as a lion. And it says here he is standing, as if ready to take action. Then John notices something unique about this Lamb: He appears to have been *slain*. The word here (*spadzo*) refers to a violent and bloody death. This is also a strong indication that Jesus' scars are still visible in heaven, an eternal reminder of the incredible sacrifice he made for you and me.

Christ is described as having "seven horns and seven eyes" (Revelation 5:6). The horns represent perfect and complete strength and authority (1 Kings 22:11; Zechariah 1:18). The seven eyes refer to the seven spirits of God, which we earlier learned are symbolic of the Holy Spirit himself and his sevenfold glory (Revelation 1:4; 4:5). The idea that the Holy Spirit is "sent out into all the earth" (Revelation 5:6) could be a reference to the Holy Spirit's ongoing ministry of convicting people of sin and bringing them to salvation during the tribulation period.

A Reason to Worship

The drama continues as next, Jesus confidently retrieves the scroll from the Father (Revelation 5:7; Daniel 7:13-14). He is now preparing to take back what is rightfully his—authority and rule over the kingdoms of the world. This act of Christ taking the scroll from the Father causes heaven to erupt into a chorus of praise. We see three such doxologies in chapter 5, and two in chapter 4. This tells us that there is spontaneous worship in heaven. Here, however, it serves as another foreboding harbinger, signally the beginning of the end of humanity. In reclaiming the planet and a people for himself, Christ must first purge the earth of evil, and he will do this by systematically destroying the strongholds of the enemy through a series of cataclysmic judgments. The wrath of God is about to fall.

In Revelation 5:8, the 4 living creatures and 24 elders fall down before the Lamb. Earlier we saw that the elders represent the church, as they have received crowns, white garments, and apparently, they have already been judged and rewarded at the bema seat (2 Corinthians 5:10; see also 1 Corinthians 3:10-15). Again, the elders are not angels because nowhere do angels sing songs of redemption. There is also no mention of elders (the church) in any of the Old Testament visions of heaven from Isaiah, Ezekiel, or Daniel. This is further compelling evidence that the elders in Revelation represent the church, the bride of Christ, whose era we see beginning in Acts 2 and ending at the rapture (1 Thessalonians 4:13-18; 2 Thessalonians 2:6-7).

The following chart clarifies this reality.

Old Testament Visions of Heaven	Revelation Vision
No elders	24 elders
No crowns/bema	Crowns/bema
No white garments	White garments
No church	Church present

As a reminder, where is the church in the book of Revelation?

Revelation 2–3   On Earth

Revelation 4–5   In heaven

Revelation 19   Returning with Christ from heaven

These elders are holding harps, which in the Old Testament are symbols of worship and prophecy (1 Samuel 10:5; 2 Kings 3:15; 1 Chronicles 25:1). This also tells us that heaven is a musical place.

The elders worship the son of God in the same way they worshipped the Father in Revelation 4:10. This is additional evidence that Jesus is God and equal to the Father. They also hold golden bowls of incense, which, in the same verse, is said to be symbolic of the prayers of the saints. Incense is elsewhere associated with prayer in Scripture (Psalm 141:2; Luke 1:9-10; Revelation 8:3-4).

It is important to recognize here that the breaking of the seals initiates God's apocalyptic judgment protocol, and it is Christ himself who breaks the seals and releases the judgments that occur at the outbreak of the tribulation (Revelation 6:1-2). This is significant because it helps determine the timing of the rapture as it relates to the seven-year tribulation itself. If the wrath of God begins with the breaking of the first seal judgment (as it clearly does in Revelation 6:1), and the church is raptured prior to the tribulation's judgments (which she clearly is—1 Thessalonians 1:10; 5:9; Revelation 3:10), then the rapture takes place *before* the tribulation. Thus, a pre-tribulational rapture.

Another reason Christ is worthy to take the scroll is because of the nature and scope of his redemption of mankind (1 Thessalonians 5:9), including people from every

tribe—ancestry/descent

tongue—language group

people—race

nation—culture

Perhaps now we understand a little bit more of what Paul meant in Colossians 1:15-16 when he wrote that "all things have been created through Him and for Him." The song the elders are singing in heaven is a song of deliverance, redemption, and rule. And it appears that only the elders are singing this song. Nowhere in the Bible are angels pictured as singing after sin enters the world (Job 38:7).[4] A careful reading of the Christmas story may alter the way angels are portrayed in most Christmas season church plays and musicals.

This redemption song reveals that part of the result of our salvation is that we are made into a "kingdom and priests" (Revelation 5:10; see also 1 Peter 2:9). That we are priests is also mentioned in Revelation 1:6 and 20:6), and elsewhere in the New Testament, we are told that we will reign with Christ (2 Timothy 2:12). This is another reason why we ascribe great praiseworthiness to the Lamb.

In Revelation 5:11, John says, "I looked," a phrase that occurs 4 times in this chapter (3 of those instances being "I saw") and 44 times total in Revelation. He says "I heard" 27 times. Truly, Revelation is an audiovisual book!

The scene John describes next is portrayed in concentric circles, with the Lamb in the center, followed by the living creatures, the elders, and the angels. He looks to see that the number of angels, combined with the redeemed and the living creatures, is innumerable. The phrase he uses is "myriads of myriads," which is the highest numerical value (10,000) John could extract from the Greek language. He simply multiplies that number by itself. It's similar to when we say "a gazillion"!

No one knows how many holy angels serve God, but we can easily calculate it to be toward a billion or more. And how would we arrive at this number?

We know from Revelation 9:16 that 200 million demons (a demonic cavalry) will plague mankind during the sixth trumpet judgment. That number, combined with the demon locusts earlier in that same chapter (the fifth trumpet judgment), along with the demons currently held in chains (2 Peter 2:4, 9; Jude 6) and those occupying Earth's atmosphere, could place the demonic number at close to half a billion. Considering that this number constitutes only one-third of the angels who originally fell with Satan (Revelation 12:4), this puts the total number of good angels easily at a billion or more. Considering the facts that angels can travel at the speed of lightning and that they have no physical atmospheric limitations, this means there are more than enough supernatural angelic beings to accomplish all of God's purposes on planet Earth (Ezekiel 1:14; Daniel 9:21-22; Luke 1:19).

And Jesus Christ is worthy to be worshipped by all of them.

The vast multitude of angels and redeemed humans around the throne join their voices together now and *say* (not sing), "Worthy is the Lamb that was slain to receive power and riches and wisdom and might and honor and glory and blessing" (Revelation 5:12).

Jesus Christ deserves all this praise. In heaven, there are no accolades too lofty or too grandiose for him. Worship in heaven it is not rote, ritualistic, or reserved. Rather, according to Revelation 5:11-12, it is wholehearted and loud—the Greek text here literally translates to "loud voice." In Revelation, at times heavenly worship is solemn (4:8, 11), while at other times it is celebratory (11:15-16; 15:3-4; 19:1-5). And it is certainly always full of emotion.

No doubt, you have experienced earthly versions of this level of enthusiasm and excitement. Perhaps that has happened

- at a football game, when a last-second winning touchdown was scored by your team
- at a wedding, when the pronouncement of marriage was made
- at a concert, when your favorite musician took the stage
- at an airport, when your military child returned home from deployment
- at a hospital, when your son or daughter was born
- at a college graduation ceremony, when that same baby later received his or her diploma

God has certainly blessed us with the wonderful gift of emotion. But as great as all our earthly experiences might be, no feeling or level of human exuberance or emotion comes remotely close to the wellspring of joy that will burst forth from your heart and heavenly lungs when you lavish praise on the one who saved your soul.

This is why Oswald Chambers wrote, "When we see him, we will wonder that we ever could have disobeyed him."[5]

That is how worthy Jesus is, my friend.

But the praise isn't finished yet! Revelation 5:13 goes on to tell us that all creation then joins in on the cheering. Essentially, the entire universe is a part of this roar of reverential worship. From this, the following is made clear to us:

- Worship is not a spectator sport. There are no back rows in heaven filled with sleepy, distracted believers. Rather, everyone participates. There is no attention deficit disorder in heaven. Everyone there is caught up in wonder and worship.

- Worship occurs only when we first respond to the truth concerning who God is. It's not emotion that leads us there, but truth. We worship, both in that day and in our own, as Jesus says, "in spirit and truth" (John 4:24). God never bypasses our minds to get to our hearts. Instead, he first engages our thinking, and then the heart. It is only then that our emotions respond properly. This is how genuine worship takes place.

- Even the unbelieving and those in hell will one day confess the unrivaled supremacy and worth of Jesus Christ (Philippians 2:9-11). And his dominion will continue for eternity, "forever and ever" (Revelation 5:13).

While all this worship is going on, the four living creatures keep on saying, "Amen" (Revelation 5:14). Translated, they are saying, "Yes, Yes, this is true, so let it be."

John then sees the elders respond by falling down and worshipping some more (verse 14). They're not done telling Jesus how great and awesome and worthy he is. They are simply in awe of his greatness.

From the narratives of Revelation chapters 4 and 5, we get the idea that worship in heaven is not static or stagnant, but active. In Revelation 4:4, the elders are sitting. Then in verse 10, they "fall down before Him." In Revelation 5:6, it is implied that they return to their seats (or perhaps are standing) in celebration at the moment when it is revealed that Jesus "has overcome" and is qualified to "open the book and its seven seals" (verse 5). After the Son receives the book from the Father, the elders fall down again while holding a harp and bowls of incense (verse 8). Perhaps they rise again, either to a sitting or standing position, in order to sing "a new song" (verses 9-10). They remain in this position until verse 14, where they fall down a third time to worship.

What strikes me here is the voluntary submission and inner compulsion to worship God. And why do they do this?

1. Because of who Christ is. This is the foundation of all worship, and worship occurs only as we expose and immerse ourselves in the truths about God that are found in his Word.

2. For what Christ has done. The more we realize the depth of our own depravity, the greater his grace and salvation will be to us. Grace is amazing only when we realize how little we deserve it. The more we understand the seriousness of our sin, the more we recognize the greatness of his grace (Romans 5:20).

3. For what Christ is going to do. Bible prophecy unveils the character and actions of God in a future context, and in this chapter, we discover that Christ

   • is worthy to break the seals of the little book and to open it (Revelation 5), meaning he is in charge of what is about to take place in Revelation 6–19.

   • still bears the physical scars of calvary in heaven, an everlasting reminder of the price he paid to redeem you and me (Revelation 5:6).

- will ensure that his saints reign with him on the earth (verse 10; 20:4)
- will receive worship from every created thing (verse 13)

All that the prophets prophesied, and all that God's children ever longed for and prayed for concerning Christ's righteousness, glory, and reign—*all of it*—will come true.

On the other hand, all that a sinful and rebellious humanity has ever dreaded—being accountable for their sins before a holy God—is also about to get very real. Their worst nightmare is about to become their present reality.

The Lamb is worthy, but the Lion is coming.

CHAPTER 7

PLANET EARTH IN PERIL

The God Who Is *Wrath*

Revelation 6–18

If Revelation is famous for anything, it is for the judgments described within. We've already seen how Jesus reproves his own bride when necessary. But in Revelation 6, the Lord turns his attention toward planet Earth and the *unredeemed*, referred to throughout as "those who dwell on the earth" (Revelation 3:10; 6:10; 8:13; 11:10 [twice]; 13:8, 12, 14 [twice]; 14:6; 17:8).

Keep in mind that at this time, the church is already in heaven, having been taken up through the rapture. God promised she would be delivered "from the wrath to come," because she is not "destined… for wrath" (1 Thessalonians 1:10; 5:9). He said she would be kept "from the hour of testing, that hour which is about to come upon the whole world" (Revelation 3:10). Now, without the restraining influence of the Holy Spirit to hold back sin and evil, a dam of depravity bursts forth, flooding the earth with a tsunami of sin (2 Thessalonians 2:6-7). With God's people gone, those who remain on earth will pursue their godless agendas unhindered. What they do not yet realize is that the creator (the one whom they claim doesn't exist) is about to pour out his wrath on them for the next seven years. But what does that mean, exactly? And what does the Bible mean by "wrath"?

There are at least five different expressions of God's wrath portrayed in Scripture.[1]

For the purposes of this chapter, we will focus on God's apocalyptic wrath. Generally speaking, God's wrath can be defined as the expression of his divine displeasure toward sin. It is his righteousness in action with regard to sin and sinners. For example, God's wrath toward sin was poured out on Jesus at the cross.[2] During his six hours of suffering, the Father not only blasted his Son with an eternity's worth of righteous anger, but also temporarily abandoned him.[3] Why? Because the wages of sin is *death*, or separation from God.[4]

And why should Christians understand God's wrath? There are several reasons: (1) It's an attribute of God—it's who he is; (2) the Bible talks about it; (3) the prospect/reality of wrath is a healthy deterrent to sin; and (4) truth about divine judgment serves as a call to salvation—a warning to flee from the coming wrath.

When God expresses his apocalyptic wrath, he will judge both humanity as a whole as well as individuals. It is in this wrath that God completely gives over those "vessels of wrath prepared for destruction" (Romans 9:22). These are the billions who have consciously and willfully crossed the line, passing through a perilous portal of no return. By repeatedly hardening their hearts, they join a rogues' gallery of rebels from the ages, including Pharaoh, Herod, and Judas.

As a part of his end-times abandonment protocol, God will send upon these people a "deluding influence so that they will believe what is false, in order that they all may be judged who did not believe the truth, but took pleasure in wickedness" (2 Thessalonians 2:11-12). This is their penalty for "not receiv[ing] the love of the truth so as to be saved" (verse 10). In the last days, the entire world will be plunged into a darkness not known since the days of Noah (Genesis 6:5). Even so, there will be a great multitude of people saved during the tribulation (see chapter 8 of this book). But for these defiant rebels, the day of hope has passed. They will become fully absorbed in their own self-worship, demonic worship, self-pursuits, and self-destruction.

But this is only half the story.

The apocalyptic wrath God now unleashes without restraint is an outpouring of fury the likes of which the world has never witnessed. Via the worldwide flood, God destroyed every living thing that breathed air in a single global event. But here, he draws out his anger over a period of seven years.

Revelation describes these end-times judgments as being divided into three series of seven judgments each: the seal judgments, the trumpet judgments, and the bowl judgments.

Let's survey these series of judgments so we can better understand what humanity will experience in the last days.

John's vision transitions now from heaven back to earth, from unending praise to undiluted fury. God will pour out wrath on the earth and its people during the seven years following the rapture, and it's almost impossible for us to grasp the magnitude and intensity of his anger. Be warned: This will be a dark chapter, but one that exalts God in his righteousness. The "hour of testing, that hour which is about to come upon the whole world" has officially arrived (Revelation 3:10).

The Seal Judgments
First Seal: Rider on a White Horse—Peace (6:1-2)

The first thing we notice in Revelation 6 is that it is *Jesus* who breaks the seals on the scroll—not man or Satan. This indicates God's wrath begins at the first seal judgment, not at the middle of the tribulation or some later date, as suggested by some.

We could define the tribulation period as seven years of God's wrath poured out upon the world prior to the second coming of Jesus and the spiritual restoration of Israel (Revelation 6:1–19:21).

When the Lamb breaks the first seal, a living creature (one of the cherubim) with a thunderous voice summons a white horse and its rider. This rider has a bow and a bestowed crown, and he goes forth "conquering and to conquer." I believe this refers to the antichrist and his ability to bring the world together in the months following the rapture. He'll do this by brokering a covenant with Israel (Daniel 9:27), and by providing something all humanity will crave at the moment—"peace and safety" (1 Thessalonians 5:1-3).

He will do this peacefully and persuasively, and without spilling a drop of blood. Scripture says he has a bow, but no arrows are mentioned. He will possess great political power—we know this because a crown will be given to him (Revelation 6:2). This harmonizes perfectly with Daniel 9:27 and the peace pact the antichrist will make with Israel, which will also officially begin the 70th week of Daniel (the seven-year tribulation). The rapture is not what starts the tribulation, but rather, antichrist's peace treaty, which will set the clock in motion.

During the first half of the tribulation, the man of sin will posture himself as a Messiah-like figure who is welcomed by the Jews and loved and lauded by the world. No doubt he will immediately be awarded the Nobel Prize for peace for accomplishing what no leader has ever done. This act will likely be a chief catalyst toward allowing the Jewish people to rebuild their temple. Muslim control of the Temple Mount will come to an abrupt end, possibly accelerated by a failed invasion of Israel, in which Islamic forces are supernaturally decimated by God himself (Ezekiel 38–39). This is also sometimes called "the War of Gog and Magog."

Hailed as a hero, the antichrist is, in reality, a *heartless* horseman.

Second Seal: Rider on a Red Horse—War (6:3-4)

Summoned by the second living creature, the rider on the red horse is given the authority to *take peace* from the earth (i.e., make war). This will mirror the violence seen on earth during the days of Noah.[5]

Antichrist's peaceful world won't last long, as the second horseman will ignite World War III. And though we are not given the details, this war will be so devastating that it triggers concentric ripple effects impacting the entire earth. In 2022, the world saw how one regional conflict—Russia's invasion of Ukraine—affected much of the planet, leading to a host of unpleasant consequences for nations thousands of miles away. This war will be exponentially worse.

Third Seal: Rider on a Black Horse—Famine (6:5-6)

When the third seal is broken, the third rider is called forth. He is on a black horse and carrying a set of scales. Because of the antichrist's actions and the war that follows, the world will be plunged into famine and poverty. One of the aftershocks of war is a shortage of food due to the destruction of crops and storage facilities, and a lack of access to supplies. Supply chains are also interrupted, preventing the delivery of goods. A voice, presumably Christ's, reveals to John the depths of this devastation: "A quart of wheat for a denarius, and three quarts of barley [normally used for animals] for a denarius."

A denarius was a first-century day's wage (Matthew 20:2). A quart of wheat was roughly equivalent to what it took to feed one person for one day. So inflation due to war (and perhaps combined with the aftershocks of life on post-rapture Earth) will drive food prices through the roof!

The inflation rate in February 2022 was 7.9 percent. During the early months of the tribulation, it will be 800 percent!

Where I live in the South, when a light snow shower occurs,

people stampede to the grocery store and stock up on food and necessities, stripping the shelves bare. Imagine the chaos and panic that will ensue when multitudes can't earn enough money to feed their families or take care of other fundamental needs.[6] Diminished food supplies won't be sufficient to meet the great demand, so prices will skyrocket. The voice John hears concludes with "do not damage the oil and the wine," both of which were staples in the first century. This indicates that famine will limit populations to eating only the basics, or perhaps that only the rich will remain unaffected.

Fourth Seal: Rider on a Pale/Ashen Horse—Death (6:8)

This horse is ashen or pale green in color, resembling the pallor of a decomposing corpse (Greek *chloros* = "pale").[7]

The rider on this horse is named Death and is accompanied by Hades (the place of the dead), and he will be given authority to kill 25 percent of Earth's population. If this were to happen today, it would be the equivalent of about 2 billion people dying. This massive death toll will be reached "with sword and with famine and with pestilence and by the wild beasts of the earth" (Revelation 2:23).[8] Jesus prophesied there will be plagues and famines during this time (Luke 21:11). Though Christ holds the keys to death and Hades (Revelation 1:13), here, he authorizes this horseman to carry out his job during this stage of the tribulation.

These four horsemen all represent effects brought on by the antichrist. And all this is merely the beginning of "birth pangs."[9]

Fifth Seal: Martyrs (6:9-11)

When Jesus breaks the fifth seal, John's eyes are diverted momentarily back to heaven, where he sees the souls of those who've been murdered for their faith during the early days of the tribulation. Specifically, they're killed because of their allegiance to the Word of God and their testimony concerning Jesus (Revelation 12:11). These souls cry out for justice but are told to wait a little while longer until the rest of their soon-to-be-martyred brethren join them in heaven.[10] This group includes those who respond to the gospel almost immediately after the rapture. They are the "left behind" who realize their tragic error of not trusting in Jesus during the church age. Perhaps they are reached through a Bible, book, video, or some other Christian resource. Or maybe the sheer terror of facing global chaos brought on by the rapture and knowing they squandered their opportunity to be saved is what ultimately drives them to their knees in repentance.

These believers will be murdered during the early part of the tribulation, long before the antichrist declares himself to be God and launches a rampage against Jews and Christians. One clue to why this happens may be found in the latter verses of Revelation 6 (which we'll look at when we get to the sixth seal).[11] During the latter days of the tribulation, believers will be beheaded for their faith (Revelation 20:4).

Sixth Seal: Cosmic Catastrophe (6:12-17)

Previously having brought judgment through the four horsemen, here, the Lord takes direct responsibility for pouring out wrath upon the earth. Though there have already been earthquakes, a massive, global seismic event will now occur (Matthew 24:7). This naturally triggers volcanic eruptions on a global scale. The resulting ash spewing into the sky will cause the sun to be darkened and the moon to resemble a blood-red hue.[12] The atmosphere itself will be altered. Asteroids and meteors will penetrate the atmosphere, colliding with the earth. Due to the unprecedented earthquake, tectonic plates will shift, realigning the earth's geography and perhaps even the continents themselves.

God will literally shake the entire planet as if to say, "Do I have your attention now?"

This will be climate change on steroids, compliments of Jesus of Nazareth.

And how will people respond?

Both rich and poor, king and slave will run for cover. Filled with fear, they will cower under rocks instead of taking shelter in the Rock of Ages).[13] They will beg the mountains to fall on them in order to shield them from "the presence of Him who sits on the throne, and from the wrath of the Lamb" (Revelation 6:15-17). There will be no doubt in anyone's mind who is responsible for these events. They will even know God's *motivation*.

The inborn God-consciousness that is present in every person will awaken and recognize that "the great day of their wrath has come, and who is able to stand?".[14] Previously, these people lived as if God didn't exist (Matthew 24:37). But now, suddenly, no one is an atheist. Following the sixth seal judgment, atheism is extinct and global terror will grip Earth's inhabitants.

Billions will admit that these judgments are from God, revealing a sobering truth: that everyone will "believe in God" during the tribulation period, acknowledging what demons have known all along (James 2:19). This highlights the utter futility of atheism, as all those who deny God's existence will face a rude awakening at the release of the seal judgments, and an even worse experience just seconds after they die. For every one of them will acknowledge the existence of God and the Lamb, both in this life and in the next.

However, because the Holy Spirit's restraining influence will have been removed by this point (2 Thessalonians 2:6-7), their collective sin natures will eventually erupt with a boiling hatred for God *because of* his judgments. Unable to launch an attack against heaven itself, it is entirely plausible that they will take out their anger and fury on those who have just become Christians, mercilessly slaughtering them during the early days and months of the tribulation. This could explain the mass martyrdom of the saints in Revelation 6:9-11.

No doubt fact checkers and philosophers—along with religious leaders, lawmakers, scientists, and heads of state—will weigh in amid the planetary panic that follows the rapture.

People will ask, "How did so many disappear? Where did they go? What caused this phenomenon?"

My belief is that initially, people will embrace all kinds of explanations that fall in the realms of demonic delusion, rumors, clickbait, and fake news. But I believe that very soon afterward, they will know it was indeed the rapture. And therefore, they will kill the new saints as fast as they can, before they can share their faith and multiply! As soon as they can be identified, they will be hunted down and murdered. They will become the scapegoats, the sacrificial lambs of the tribulation. And so, it appears that even pagans in that day will believe in a pre-tribulation rapture!

The Trumpet Judgments

At the breaking of the seventh seal (Revelation 8:1), there will be silence in heaven for half an hour (like the silence before a courtroom verdict is read).

John has heard a lot so far, including thunder (4:5); praise (4:8); angels' voices (5:2); choruses of praise (5:9-13); angels summoning four horsemen (6:1, 3, 5, 7), and a great multitude of saints, angels, and elders praising God (7:9-13).

Here, there is 30 minutes of silence. Most likely it is because those in heaven are contemplating the gravity of what is about to happen—like the calm before the storm. This will be a sobering half hour (Psalm 76:8-9; Habakkuk 2:20; Zephaniah 1:7; 2:13).

Next, seven angels will be given seven trumpets (8:2). These are angels "who stand" before God. "Stand" is in the perfect tense, indicating they have been there for some time. Some have called them "presence angels," and Gabriel is likely one of them (Luke 1:19). Other passages in Scripture describe angels as assisting God in delivering judgment (Matthew 13:39-41, 45-50; 16:27; 25:31).

"Another angel" is seen standing at the altar with a golden censer (8:3). Is this Jesus in his priestly role? Is it the angel of Yahweh? (Genesis 16:7; Exodus 3:2; Numbers 22:22; Judges 2:1). Probably not, since Jesus is identified as the "Lamb" (Revelation 6:1). Here, much incense is given to him to add to the prayers of the saints at the golden altar that is before the throne. This is the same altar that Isaiah and Ezekiel saw in Isaiah 6:6 and Ezekiel 10:2. In the Old Testament, the altar was nearest to the Holy of Holies (Exodus 30:3-6). Here, it's near the throne (the presence of God), and the "How long, O Lord" prayer of Revelation 6:9-10 is about to begin being answered.

The angel takes the censer, fills it with fire, and throws it to the earth (Revelation 8:4-5). It is seen as a massive fireball from the sky. Thunder and lightning follow, accompanied by a major earthquake. This is the second earthquake that is mentioned in Revelation (6:12).

Next, seven angels appear, prepared to blow their trumpets (Revelation 8:6).

Trumpet Blast #1: Ecological Disaster—Bloody Hail and Fire (8:7)

In the Old Testament, trumpets were used to call people to gather (Numbers 10:2), direct soldiers to war (Numbers 10:9; 2 Chronicles 13:17), and on the first of the month and on special occasions. But here, they release hail, fire, and blood from the sky to the earth. Hail and fire mingled with blood were often associated with divine judgment (Genesis 19:24; Exodus 9:13-15; 38:22; Job 38:22-23; Psalms 11:6; 105:32; Joel 2:30—the day of the Lord). The cause of the hail and fire could be the earthquake that had just occurred. Some have speculated that the "fire mingled with blood" could refer to flaming lava. Atmospheric disturbances caused by volcanic eruptions could also produce violent thunderstorms with hail. The blood mentioned here could also result from people and animals being catapulted into the sky by eruptions. The result? One-third of the earth will be scorched, including one-third of all trees (see Revelation 7:2-3). And *all* the green grass will be burned up ("green grass" meaning all green grass growing at the time of this judgment—note Revelation 9:4, where demons are not allowed to hurt the grass).[15]

The fire from this judgment will also cause catastrophic wildfires. Crops, forests, vegetation, and wildlife will all be threatened.

This will be a global catastrophe, and it will cause massive destruction to the earth's vegetation. This will be a different kind of Earth Day on God's calendar. And he will scorch the planet thoroughly.

Trumpet Blast #2: A Flaming Mountain Crashes into the Ocean (8:9)

John says this will be "like" a burning mountain, so this probably refers to an asteroid or a giant meteor. The result? A truly doomsday scenario.

One-third of the sea will become blood. Much of Earth's oxygen comes from phytoplankton and algae in the world's oceans, and from the rainwater that falls as a result of evaporation from the oceans. With the oceans contaminated by this burning mountain, Earth's oxygen supply will be affected. One-third of the creatures in the sea will die. This could partly explain why the sea resembles blood. The smoke from volcanic eruptions will cause the sun to have a reddish hue, which might add to the reddish glow on all the waters. One-third of the ships worldwide will be destroyed. They will likely be sunk by massive tsunamis caused by the burning mountain crashing into the sea.

According to marinetraffic.com, there are 172,277 legally registered ships in the world that are more than 65 feet in length. For one-third of them to be destroyed comes to 57,000 large ships. Commerce and transport will suddenly be devastated, causing the world's economy to collapse.

Trumpet Blast #3: Earth's Fresh Water Supply Contaminated (8:10-11)

A great star named Wormwood will fall from heaven, burning like a torch and affecting one-third of the rivers and one-third of the springs of waters. These waters will become "wormwood," and many people will die from the waters because they were made bitter. "Wormwood" is used only in the New Testament; it refers to a plant whose leaves are used to make absinthe.[16]

But here in Revelation, it's lethal.

That the catastrophic events we've looked at occur in thirds is evidence that they are of divine origin, and not merely random meteorological events.

Another immediate aftershock of this judgment is that many people will die. Remember, by this time, people will already be starving in parts of the world because of famines that struck earlier (6:8-9).

But when rivers, wells, springs, lakes, and reservoirs become poisoned, starvation rates will increase dramatically.

All this makes one wonder if there will be deadly skirmishes and battles between people fighting over possession of clean, uncontaminated water.

Trumpet Blast #4: Light of the Heavens Darkened (8:12-13)

In this judgment, one-third of the light on planet Earth will be "smitten." One-third of the sun, one-third of the moon, and one-third of the stars will be dimmed. God will cause a "planetary power outage," as if to declare, "It is I who controls the light and the waters, the grass and the seas."

This reduction of light could refer to a partial eclipse of the sun, or some other divine means of dimming the light that reaches the earth. Whatever the case, we know it is temporary because later, in Revelation 16:8-9, God will turn up the sun and its heat, with people being scorched. However, when the lights of the heavens are darkened, the loss of heat will likely send temperatures plummeting. This will disrupt the world's weather patterns, leading to violent storms and erratic tides. More crops and people will surely die.[17]

Next, an eagle, probably an angel (cf. Revelation 4:7), will appear, flying in mid-heaven, declaring with a loud voice, "Woe, woe, woe to those who dwell on the earth, because of the remaining blasts of the trumpet of the three angels who are about to sound." He will announce three woes, one for each remaining trumpet judgment. The word "woe" is one of grief, denunciation, judgment, or long-overdue punishment (Matthew 11:21; it also appears eight times in Matthew 23, in verses 13, 14, 15, 16, 23, 25, 27, 29). Here again, we see the phrase "those who dwell on the earth" referring to those who reject the gospel (3:10; 6:10; 8:13; 11:10 [twice]; 13:8, 12, 14 [twice]; 14:6; 17:8; see also 13:3, 7, 16). These billions are "tested" (exposed to judgment) partly in order to vindicate God's later condemnation of them, as not a single person in this massive throng will repent (see Revelation 6:15-17; 9:20-21; 16:9, 11, 21).

Revelation 8 provides a prime reason why mankind should not worship the world: because as it turns out, Mother Earth has a Father *and* a creator. And he is going to bring unimaginable ecological upheaval upon her. The entire climate change movement will have officially died by this point—mainly because there is nothing people can do to stop God's judgments. He will continue destroying one of humanity's chief idols: creation itself. And because God made the earth, speaking it into existence, it is his to do with as he pleases (Genesis 1:1; Psalms 24:1; 115:3).

Trumpet Blast #5: Flying Demon Locust Scorpions (9:1-12)

In this first woe, a "star," here a fallen angel, takes a key, opening "the bottomless pit," which is home to a vile brand of demonic creatures.[18]

This "star" is not an inanimate object, but rather, personified (see "him" and "he" in verses 1-2, and Genesis 6:2; Job 1:6; 2:1; 38:7, where "stars" are the "sons of God").

But who could this "star" be? Possibly Satan (Isaiah 14:12-15).

A key is given to him that opens a "bottomless pit," or the abode of demons—a place of punishment for especially wicked fallen angels (Luke 8:31; 2 Peter 2:4; Jude 6-7). We see this pit mentioned seven times in Revelation (9:1, 2, 11; 11:7; 17:8; 20:1, 3). In Luke 8:28, the demons beg Jesus not to send them into "the abyss," where they would be tormented.[19]

After the fall, God sent the promise of a woman who would give birth to one who would destroy Satan and deliver people from his power (Genesis 3:15). Satan countered by sending demons to cohabitate with mortal women, attempting to produce a hybrid demonic-human race of people for whom God could not atone (Genesis 6:1-4). Presumably, a large number of demons and women participated in this satanic sexual activity. Obviously, Satan's plan was for this to spread globally. This hybrid race would have been created in a demonic image, not God's.

They were unsuccessful.

It's possible some of the demons in Revelation 9 include those who cohabited with mortal women in the days of Noah, prompting God to keep them in chains for more than 5,000 years.[20]

Next, smoke bellows out from the abyss and darkens the sky above (verses 2-3) as these hideous creatures appear. They are described as locusts with stinger tails like scorpions (verses 3, 5, 10). And they fly, which enables them to go fast. For *five straight months* (the normal life span of locusts) they are given authority to torment (but not kill) mankind. However, those who have God's seal of salvation on them will be protected (2 Timothy 2:19; Revelation 3:12; 22:4).

The strike of these demon locusts is compared to a scorpion's painful sting. John uses the word "like" ten times in this passage. He pictures them as horses prepared for battle, with man-faces and golden crown-like headgear, perhaps representing their intelligence and ability to conquer. They have lions' teeth and long hair (both hideous and seductive). Their breastplates are like iron, offering protection, and the collective swarming sound of their wings resembles that of horses or chariots rushing to battle. And they are filled with fury and hatred for God and the human beings he made in his image. Their pleasure is found in tormenting mankind. This is what demons would do to everyone, if allowed. These scorpion-locust demons attack at will in a full-on torture-frenzy. The physical pain and psychological horror they inflict will be so intense that people will beg to die but won't be able to.[21] They will experience a foretaste of hell in that both suicide and relief will be denied them (and consider that these people will be given five months to repent!).

A king called the "angel of the abyss" will lead these demons. In Hebrew, his name is *Abaddon*. In Greek, it's *Apollyon*. In English, it's *Destroyer*. This is the only place in Scripture where these two words are found. This is probably a high-ranking sub-angel.

This should be sufficient reason to make sure you are not left behind at the rapture. And it's only the first of three woes.

Trumpet Blast #6: Demonic Cavalry of 200 Million (9:13-21)

At the start of this second woe, John hears a voice coming from the altar before God. This voice commands the sixth angel to release the four demons who have been bound at the Euphrates River (this area is the origin of sin, murder, Babel, and globalism).[22] These could be the demons who controlled Babylon, Medo-Persia, Greece, and Rome (Daniel 10:13—"Prince of Persia"). The four fallen angels were "prepared," much as the fish was "appointed" to swallow Jonah (Jonah 1:17). This reminds us that God has supreme authority over both demons and nature.

These four devils have been held captive specially for this exact day, to be released upon the earth.[23] So sovereign is our God that he even uses demons to fulfill his righteous purposes. Their mission? To kill another third of mankind (death's five-month vacation will end at this time). At this time, a little more than half of the earth's population will have been destroyed![24] Imagine disposing of more than three billion bodies! Consider the stench, disease, sorrow, and anguish.

John tells us these four foul demonic generals will convene to lead an army numbered at 200 million. Yes, you read that right: *200 million.*

John reaffirms this fact by saying he actually "heard" the number with his own ears (Revelation 9:16). Bible teachers have suggested several interpretations as to who this army is. Many say it refers to the Chinese military, since China has, for decades, boasted of fielding a force this size. But though Revelation 6 tells us God previously used human armies to accomplish his purposes, these don't appear to be ordinary horses and horsemen, as they're associated with demons. The mounted cavalry here are wearing a supernatural armor of fire, sulfur, and brimstone (verses 17-18).[25] And the fire-breathing demon horses have tails like serpents, and "with them they do harm" (verse 19).

But just how do these four armies kill people? Verse 18 tells us this happens by...

- fire—they burn people to death
- smoke—their victims will die by asphyxiation
- brimstone—this is a sulfurous, burning rock (see Genesis 19:24; Luke 17:29) and a foretaste of the lake of fire (Revelation 14:10; 19:20; 20:10; 21:8)[26]

By this time during the tribulation, this will be the worst single judgment on humanity since Noah's flood.

What about those who survive the attacks by these hellish horsemen? In a clear display of the human heart's wickedness, amazingly, these people will not repent (Revelation 9:20-21), even when confronted with God's repeated judgments.[27] Shades of Pharaoh, right? Though half of the world will have been destroyed, people still won't be convinced of their need for salvation. Instead, they will harden their hearts and continue "to worship demons" and inanimate, mute idols made of gold, silver, brass, stone, and wood (verse 20).

The veneration of manmade idols is often associated with demonic worship.[28] This highlights the fact that we're all natural-born worshippers. We simply cannot *not* worship something. Rather, we irresistibly pursue that which gives us a perceived sense of meaning, identity, love, or comfort. And a darkened, hardened, godless heart will seek those things through the most corrupt means possible. That is why God's first commandment under Moses' leadership was, "You shall have no other gods before Me," immediately followed by "You shall not make for yourself an idol...You shall not worship them or serve them" (Exodus 20:3-5).

For all our technology and sophistication, left alone, we are powerless to rise above our inborn sin and paganism. During the end times, humanity will not have moved beyond its ancient counterpart. Whether living in a desert tent 4,000 years ago or in a highrise condo today, not much has changed about us. Both then and now, we naturally resist God and embrace darkness.[29] Though some people during tribulation may initially exhibit respectable religiosity, it appears there will also be a strong resurgence in the worship of demonic entities. Allegiance to these demons will be visually represented through sculpted or carved images made of stone, wood, and precious metals.

With God's restrainer absent during this time, demons will have a field day. They will be unchecked and unimpeded by the Holy Spirit's presence in the bride of Christ, who will have been raptured. As a result, demons' ability to oppress humans will exponentially increase. It's ironic that the remaining earth-dwellers will worship the very demons who bring their pain and suffering. Such is the deceptive trickery of sin, Satan, and the human heart. And it's the ultimate form of slavery. In short, sin makes people stupid (Romans 1:21-22).

Revelation 9 closes by saying that mankind will stubbornly refuse to repent of their sins, including murder, sorcery, immorality, and theft (verse 21). In a world gone mad, men and women desperately reach out for anything promising survival or satisfaction.

1. *Murders*—During the tribulation, the murder rate will soar as a spirit of chaos envelops the world.

2. *Sorceries*—The word translated "sorceries" here is the Greek word *pharmakon* and can refer to anything from poisons, amulets, charms, drugs, magic spells, and witchcraft to any enchanting object.[30] Drugs were heavily used in first-century sorcery, inducing a psychological state conducive to trances for contacting departed or demonic spirits. This practice will become prevalent during the last days.[31]

   As our world continues racing toward Revelation, expect to see drug use and abuse continue to rise and become legal. And in the turmoil and madness of the tribulation, drug use will reach epidemic levels. People will seek to escape into a drug-bunker of protection from the world outside their door and retreat into an insulated, hallucinogenic, mind-numbing haze.

3. *Immorality*—People will also practice unrestrained

immorality, just as they did in Noah's day and in Sodom and Gomorrah.[32] Gay marriage, transgenderism, and polyamory will increase. Some now are pushing for pedophilia to be decriminalized, reclassifying offenders from "perverts" to "minor-attracted individuals."[33] Even now, sexual taboos are being removed both officially and in the public psyche. Heinous sins are being reclassified as disorders. Unnatural sexual orientations are accepted, supported, protected, celebrated, and even honored. All this is setting the stage and preparing what's left of the human race for utter decadence in the end times.[34]

4. *Thefts*—During the tribulation, crime will reach unprecedented proportions. Lawlessness will run rampant. The looting and thievery that takes place will make today's violent riots and crime rates seem like a church picnic. Anarchy will fill the earth, and no home or individual will be safe. "What's yours is mine!" will become the new Main Street mantra.

Demon worship. Idolatry. Murders. Sorceries. Immorality. Thefts. This is the moral "weather forecast" for humanity during the tribulation. People will commit these sins for security and to survive, all the while refusing to repent. In doing so, they will birth within themselves a violent spirit of hatred toward God that we'll see more of later in Revelation.[35] This is the deceptive danger of harboring a hard heart toward God.[36]

Before moving on to the final set of judgments, by way of review, we've seen that

- humanity isn't getting better and will become more depraved following the rapture (Jeremiah 17:9; 2 Thessalonians 2:10-12; Revelation 16:10-11)

- God's judgments will become more acute and severe as the tribulation progresses
- God's sovereignty enables him to use even demons and evil to accomplish his purposes

Trumpet Blast #7—Includes the Bowl Judgments (11:15-19)

This final trumpet judgment also includes the seven bowl judgments, as both are portrayed as finishing up God's wrath on mankind during the tribulation (Revelation 11:15-17; 16:17). Because both the seventh trumpet and the seven bowls are said to complete God's wrath, the bowls must be part of the seventh trumpet judgment.

This also marks the end of the interlude that lasts from Revelation 10:1–11:14.

In addition, the seventh trumpet introduces the third woe (the first is the demon locusts in Revelation 8:13 and 9:3-12; the second is the army of 200 million demons in Revelation 9:13-21; 11:14; and the third includes all seven bowl judgments).

We should also note that the seventh trumpet is not the same as the "last trumpet" in 1 Corinthians 15:52.[37]

Now, the judgments associated with the seventh trumpet are not described until Revelation chapter 15. In Revelation chapters 12–14 are vignettes that provide other information about the tribulation, including details about the antichrist.

During the tribulation, God's wrath will come "to destroy those who destroy the earth" (Revelation 11:18). This is a play on words, where the same word ("destroy") can literally mean "to destroy" and "to corrupt." God is saying that he will destroy those who have corrupted the earth with their immorality (see Revelation 19:2). This is not God punishing mankind for polluting the earth with fossil fuel emissions or other environmental "offenses," but rather, this is a vindictive response to those who have stained God's earth with their *sin*.

The Seven Bowl Judgments (Revelation 16:1-21)

This final series of judgments will occur during the last three-and-a-half years of the tribulation. Seven special angels will be summoned to the precipice of heaven and will pour out the most intense of all God's judgments thus far.

Bowl Judgment #1—Painful Sores (16:2)

God will single out a group of people for this judgment: those who have taken "the mark of the beast" (Revelation 16:2; 19:20). That will include everyone on the planet who didn't trust in Jesus as Savior. Upon receiving the mark, their destiny will be eternally sealed (Revelation 14:9-11). We know this judgment will take place during the second half of the tribulation because it falls on those who have taken the mark, which won't go into effect until after the midpoint of the tribulation, when the abomination of desolation occurs (Daniel 9:27; Matthew 24:15; 2 Thessalonians 2:3-4; Revelation 13:3-18).

These sores are described as "loathsome and malignant" (Revelation 16:2). They will be painful and incurable. The word "sore" comes from the Greek *kelkos*, which, when translated into Latin, gives us the English term we know as *ulcer*.[38]

Some think these sores represent radiation poisoning from nuclear detonation (see Revelation 8:7). More likely, they will result from supernatural judgment that could occur at the time people receive the mark of the beast. Though this is a temporal judgment on those who worship the beast, eternal judgment will come upon them as well (14:9-11).

Bowl Judgment #2—Oceans Contaminated (16:3)

The second angel will pour his bowl upon the seas, which will become "blood like that of a dead man" (verse 3). Everything in the oceans will die, and the resulting stench will be unimaginable (if you have ever smelled a dead fish or rat, you can get some idea of what it will be like). Multiply this by billions of creatures, and you know the smell will be unbearable. This judgment is similar to that which took place at the second trumpet judgment (Revelation 8:8-9), when one-third of the sea became blood and one-third of the creatures died. It is also similar to the first of the ten plagues upon ancient Egypt.

The putrid odor will no doubt permeate all coastal areas, with the smell being blown inland by winds.

Bowl Judgment #3—Rivers and Fresh Water Become Blood (16:4)

Virtually all drinking water will be contaminated. This, combined with the second bowl judgment, will contribute to an environmentalist's worst nightmare. The fresh water supply will already be critically low by this time (8:10-11) due to the third trumpet judgment, when one-third of the waters in the world's rivers become poisonous. After this bowl judgment, there will be hardly any drinkable water on the planet.

Further exacerbating this is that the two witnesses who possess the power to stop the rain will also have turned the waters into blood (11:6). This judgment will cause unthinkable hardship and suffering. Not only will there be no water to drink or to cook with, but also none for people to use to relieve or wash their painful sores.

And what kind of God would do this? The same passage gives us the answer:

- a righteous God, who is also eternal and holy (Revelation 16:5).

- a just God (verse 6), who is delivering payback for spilling the blood of the saints and the prophets (two witnesses). It's as if God is saying, "You like blood. Here's some for you!"

It is not conceivable that everyone on the earth will participate in the killing of Christians. But apparently even those who stand by and do nothing, or who applaud those who do kill, will be just as guilty. This is made clear in verse 6, which concludes with these chilling words: "They deserve it."

Those around the altar in heaven will "amen" this judgment—they will say, "Yes, O Lord God, the Almighty, true and righteous are Your judgments" (verse 7). The people and altar here may be the same whom we see in Revelation 6:9, the martyred saints, who were murdered and are pictured there as being protected under the altar of God.

Bowl Judgment #4—Scorching Heat (16:8-9)

When the fourth trumpet was blown, one-third of the sun was darkened (Revelation 8:12). There was also a prelude to darkness in the sixth seal judgment (6:12), probably because of the volcanic ash that resulted from eruptions after a great earthquake. But here, the sun *increases* its intensity, to the point that the searing heat burns those on the earth.[39]

Again, what is undeniable here is that a specific group is singled out—that is, "the people" (translated "men" in verse 8-9). There is a definite article before the noun, indicating that only this group suffers. It's the same group we see in verses 2, 5, and 6. And it's the same group we see in verse 9, referred to as "they."

So intense is this heat that it will be as if the air itself is on fire. This will surely melt the polar ice caps. Oceans will rise dramatically, flooding coastal areas for miles inland and bringing bloody, putrid water along with massive damage and loss of property and life. This will only add to the unspeakable misery people are already experiencing. It would also presumably impact commercial transportation on the ocean, though not nearly as severe as we will see in Revelation 18:17.

And what will be humanity's cumulative respond to these four judgments? "They blasphemed the name of God who has the power over these plagues, and they did not repent so as to give Him glory" (Revelation 16:9). This is the first record of people blaspheming God in the book of Revelation. Previously, only the antichrist blasphemed God (Revelation 13:1, 5-6). This shows us the influence antichrist's rule will have on humanity. Tragically, billions of people will be

- deceived by the antichrist (Matthew 24:4-5; 2 Thessalonians 2:9-10),
- deluded by God (2 Thessalonians 2:11), and
- destined to condemnation by their refusal to repent (Revelation 14:9-11; 16:9).

Sadly, many people will ignore the warning sent through the rapture. They will reject the gospel proclaimed to them through God's servants. And even the outpouring of God's wrath will not convince people to repent (Revelation 9:20-21).

Bowl Judgment #5—Darkness (16:10-11)

This judgment will be poured out on "the throne of the beast," which refers to the antichrist's kingdom. Similar to the ninth plague upon ancient Egypt, it will likely be "a darkness which may be *felt*" (Exodus 10:21-23).

All of antichrist's kingdom will go black. This will be more than just a power grid failure; it will be a supernatural phenomenon. There will be such mental anguish and insanity resulting from the darkness that people will gnaw their tongues in emotional agony (Revelation 16:10). The verb tense here indicates that they "kept on chewing." Imagine the kind of mental pain that could cause such torment.

However, instead of falling to their knees, people will stiffen their necks. They will blaspheme God, all the while refusing to "repent of their deeds" (verse 11).

Bowl Judgment #6—Euphrates River Dries Up (16:12-16)

This great river will go dry in preparation for the "kings from the east" to make their way toward Armageddon. The Euphrates River formed the eastern boundary of the ancient Roman Empire and the land God had promised to Abraham's seed (Genesis 15:18). Though there are more than 50 different interpretations as to who these kings of the east are, it is best to understand them as including China and any other Eastern nations that are a part of the antichrist's coalition.[40]

Then three demons will perform signs that seduce the kings of the whole world "to gather them together for the war of the great day of God, the Almighty" (Revelation 16:14). And where will these demons lead them? "To the place which in Hebrew is called Har-Magedon" (verse 16).

Bowl Judgment #7—Global Destruction (16:17-21)

This final judgment will be poured out "upon the air," and will be preceded by a loud voice from the temple and the throne, saying, "It is done" (verse 17). It will be followed by flashes of lightning and peals of thunder. Then a massive earthquake will occur, the biggest to ever hit planet Earth. So big, even the Richter scale won't be able to measure it.

The result of this colossal earthquake will be the destruction of the "great city," Babylon, which is the antichrist's headquarters. When it comes to unforgiven sin, God has a long memory; therefore, he will pour out his fury on that place (verse 19). All the chief cities of the nations will also fall at this time. Worldwide destruction will occur, including the disintegration of every island and mountain (verse 20).

This will be followed by 100-pound hailstones raining down from heaven, described in verse 21 as "extremely severe."

And the response from those upon the earth? "Men blasphemed God" (verse 21).

All of this is part of the wrath Paul spoke about in 1 Thessalonians 1:10 and 5:9. It is terrible, horrific, unbearable, and unquestionably from God.

But during the seven-year tribulation, will there be any who respond to God's call to salvation? Will any become saved? Will God still extend his grace?

Revelation gives us the answer in the next chapter.

CHAPTER 8

THE LAST GREAT AWAKENING

The God Who Is *Gracious*

Revelation 6:6-11; 7:1-17; 11:1-14; 14:6-7; 20:4

One of the most-asked questions I get is, "Do you see a great revival taking place in the last days before the rapture?" And I understand why people want to know. After all, there have been similar awakenings in the past:

- The Great Reformation in Europe during the sixteenth century, when giants like John Calvin and Martin Luther championed a return to the Scriptures and salvation by grace alone instead of works.

- The Great Awakening in eighteenth-century America, when revival swept the country through men like George Whitfield and Jonathan Edwards. So prevalent was the spiritual awakening that, according to Benjamin

Franklin, "It seemed as if all the world were growing religious; so that one could not walk through the town in an evening without hearing psalms sung in different families of every street."[1]

- The Welsh Revival of the early twentieth century saw even the vilest of sinners converted, including the earthy, vulgarity-spewing coal miners of the day. They would ride their donkeys each day to the coal mines, swearing and cursing commands at them. But upon their conversions to Christ, the men no longer cursed at their donkeys, causing the animals to become confused. The result was that they wouldn't move anymore![2]

Can we expect a comparable revival in these last days? Does the Bible give us any hints or clues regarding such a future awakening? As we survey end-times prophecies, we discover that no such revival is prophesied. What *is* prophesied, however, is a last-days apostasy, or a falling away from the faith (2 Thessalonians 2:3; 1 Timothy 4:1; 2 Timothy 3:1-9).

This of course, doesn't mean there can't or won't be a great awakening prior to the rapture. It just means we don't see one prophesied in Scripture.

However, in passages about the tribulation period, we do see great numbers of people coming to faith in Jesus. So, yes, there is a great harvest coming, only it will take place after the rapture. So what will happen, and how?

The revivals of the past have all taken place in the midst of dark and sometimes depressing times. And the future faith awakening is no exception to this pattern. The tribulation period will be a time that witnesses not only the unprecedented outpouring of God's furious wrath against humanity (Revelation 6–19), but also a depth of depravity not seen since the days of Noah. It is then, in the midst of divine judgment, that the vast majority of humankind will not only harden their hearts against God, but stubbornly and defiantly do so. They will even repeatedly blaspheme him while refusing to repent of their sin, immorality, and demon worship (Revelation 9:20-21; 16:9, 11; see also 2 Thessalonians 2:10-12). They will go so far as to vow their allegiance to the antichrist, venerating him as God almighty (Revelation 13:3-17).

It is during this dismal time that God's grace will shine forth to birth a redeemed remnant.

Those Who Are Left Behind Believe

We first read about this massive number of end-times believers in Revelation 6:9-11. The people we see in this scene are among the firstfruits of the tribulation. They will come to faith early on as evidenced by the fact they are already in heaven during the very first set of tribulation judgments. From the pattern we see throughout Revelation, it appears as if mankind, on the whole, will grow progressively more defiant against God as time goes by (6:16-17; 9:20-21; 14:9-11). The masses will resist the promptings of God and refuse to repent, eventually reaching a point where God will abandon them to their sin and irreversible destiny (Romans 1:18-32; Revelation 14:9-11).

Because this pattern of unbelief worsens as the tribulation wears on, it is highly probable that the vast majority of those who come to Christ will do so during the first three-and-a-half years. Further evidence of this is that anyone caught believing in Jesus and refusing the mark of the beast during the second half of the tribulation will be, for the most part, martyred by beheading under the antichrist's tyrannical rule (Revelation 20:4).

So, those who become believers during the first half of the tribulation may come to faith fairly quickly after the rapture. Remember, the rapture will not officially begin the seven-year tribulation. Rather, the signing of a peace covenant between Israel and the antichrist is what will begin the prophetic seven-year clock (Daniel 9:27). Conceivably, there may be weeks, or even several months, between the rapture of the church and the start of the seven-year tribulation.

During this interlude, panic and chaos will blanket the earth. In the midst of economic collapse, violence and looting, anarchy in the streets, emotional breakdowns, suicides, geopolitical upheavals, and the threats of war, God will continue calling his elect to himself (Ephesians 1:4; Romans 9–11). Not only are these first believers in Revelation 6 represented in this end-times group of martyrs, but countless others will eventually join them from every corner of the world. Revelation 7:9-10 states,

> After these things I looked, and behold, a great multitude which no one could count, from every nation and all tribes and peoples and tongues, standing before the throne and before the Lamb, clothed in white robes, and palm branches were in their hands; and they cry out with a loud voice, saying, "Salvation to our God who sits on the throne, and to the Lamb."

John declares their number to be incalculable. They come from every nation (culture), tribe (descent), people (race), and tongue (language group). It is a massive harvest! But the point here isn't so much the *diversity* of those saved, but rather, the great *mercy* of God. He is no respecter of race, but he is also a rescuer of sinners, no matter who or where they may be.

Again, this includes the martyrs in Revelation 6. But Revelation 7:9-10 provides a more wide-angle view of the extent of God's grace during the tribulation. Some of these people are no doubt a part of those mentioned in Revelation 20:4 as having been beheaded for not receiving the antichrist's mark on their forehead or right hand.

So we can say with confidence that a great multitude will be saved during the tribulation, and most likely during the first half. We know they will go straight into God's presence upon death (Revelation 7:9, 13-14). They will be declared righteous before him (verse 9). They will participate in loud and joyous worship upon their arrival (verse 10-12). They will enjoy close proximity to God's throne and serve him day and night in his temple (verse 15). And they will be forever protected by the Father and relieved of every earthly pain and sorrow associated with their former life (verses 16-17).

Salvation During the Tribulation

This brings us to another question: *How* will they be saved? Let's address that question three ways: by looking at the *manner*, the *methods*, and the *means* of their salvation experience.

1. The Manner

People often ask, "If the Holy Spirit is removed at the rapture, how will people become saved during the tribulation?" To be clear, the Holy Spirit himself will not leave planet Earth along with the bride of Christ at the rapture. Only his unique ministry of restraining sin and holding back the appearance of the antichrist is what will be removed (2 Thessalonians 2:6-7). Because he is God, and thus omnipresent (everywhere at once), the Holy Spirit cannot be absent from the earth. His presence is simultaneously here, all over the universe, and even in hell (Psalm 139:7-12; Jeremiah 23:24).

But even though the Spirit's restraining influence through the church will have ceased, his ministry of convicting people of sin and their need for Christ will continue (John 16:8-11). In fact, no one can come to faith in Jesus unless God first draws that person to himself (John 6:44, 65). So the Holy Spirit will not be absent from Earth. He will be here, working with the Father to convict people of their need for Jesus and salvation.

Because the church age is unique and will conclude with the rapture, there is some reason to believe the Holy Spirit's relationship to the tribulation saints will be more akin to that of the Old Testament saints' experience in terms of his indwelling and service (compare 1 Samuel 16:14; 18:12; and Psalm 51:11 with John 14:16-17). Further, the tribulation is primarily concerned with God's dealings with Israel as a nation. This has led some scholars to conclude that the Holy Spirit's relationship with these new believers "will exclude indwelling and filling in the same way the bride of Christ experience these ministries."[3] So he will be with them, just not in them, as he was with the church.

However, Jesus will still "save forever" (Hebrews 7:25) all those who place faith in him during the tribulation.

2. The Methods

So how will people hear about Jesus during the tribulation if all the Christians are gone? Because of God's amazing grace, he will make the gospel known in a variety of ways. Here are some of them:

Previous Exposure to the Gospel

Some unbelievers will have memories of past experiences during which the seed of truth was planted in their hearts—through a pastor, parent, or peer who shared Christ with them. In the pandemonium that takes place after the rapture, God will bring to their minds those conversations and other encounters with the gospel. This will drive them to repentance and faith in Christ. It is also likely that many will be saved within minutes of realizing that millions have suddenly disappeared from Earth.

Gospel Resources That Are Left Behind

Only Christians themselves will be raptured—not their Bibles, books, videos, or recordings. The printed and digital materials that exist at the time of the rapture will remain and will be stumbled upon or even sought out by those whose hearts are broken and convicted. The Father and the Spirit will place these resources in the paths of these future saints.

The 144,000 Jewish Evangelists

Because the vast multitude of recently saved people are mentioned in the verses immediately following the description of the 144,000 Jewish evangelists, it makes sense to conclude that one is responsible for the other. In other words, God will use these evangelists to bring millions to faith during the tribulation. But who are these evangelists? And what can we know about their identity and ministry?

Their Number—Scripture specifically states there will be exactly 144,000 of them. John first hears the number (Revelation 7:4) and later actually *sees* them (14:1). There is no contextual reason to suggest this number is symbolic or representative of something else (as the 24 elders are in Revelation 4:4). Jesus is being literal and numerically precise here, just as he was with the seven churches (Revelation 1:11), the seven pastors (1:20), the four living creatures (4:6), the seven seals (5:1; 6:1), one-fourth of the earth's population dying (6:8), the four angels (7:1), the seven trumpets (8:1-2), the 200 million horsemen (9:16), the two witnesses (11:3), the number 666 (13:18), the seven bowls (16:1), and the 1,000-year reign of Christ (20:2-7).

Their Divisions—There will be 12,000 of these Jewish men from each of the 12 tribes of Israel (7:5-8).

Their Ethnicity—These evangelists will come "from every tribe of the sons of Israel" (7:4). That's pretty clear. "Israel" appears 66 times in the New Testament, and in every instance, it refers to the Jews, never to Gentiles or the church. These men are all racial descendants of Jacob (Israel). The church and the nation of Israel are never mixed up in the New Testament, though individual Jews can be part of the church (Galatians 3:26).

Their Character—The Bible says these Jewish men are sexually pure, and all of them are virgins (Revelation 14:4). The word "chaste" is *parthenos* in the Greek language and means "virgin." They will not have been "defiled with women" (had sexual contact or engaged in sexual activity). Their hearts, minds, and bodies will be pure. This is impressive considering the rampant immorality that will saturate humanity during this time (Revelation 9:21).

These men will be of impeccable character. Like Daniel, there will be no dirt on them (see Daniel 6:4). They will be men of integrity, with "no lie…found in their mouth" (Revelation 14:5). They will tell the truth and refuse to compromise their character.

Their Allegiance—They will be fiercely devoted to Jesus the Messiah and "follow the Lamb wherever he goes" (Revelation 14:4). This tells us Christ will minister through these servants; they will be loyal to him. In spite of worldly pressure, these Jews won't budge in their obedience to their Lord—like Shadrach and his friends in Daniel 3. In Revelation 7:3, the 144,000 are called the "bond-servants of our God."

Their Salvation—John describes these evangelists as being "purchased from among men as first fruits to God and to the Lamb" (Revelation 14:4). This means they will be among the first to be saved during the tribulation. The word "purchased" is used two times in verses 3-4, indicating that they belong to the Lamb. Because they are the firstfruits, this is evidence of a great future harvest of souls during the tribulation (7:9).

Their Ministry—It is strongly inferred that the 144,000 in Revelation 7:1-8 are directly connected to the salvation of the "great multitude" in verse 9. Further, the fact that they are the firstfruits among those who are saved also links them to a ministry of evangelism. Put plainly, the 144,000 exist to follow Christ and tell the world about him. They have no other ambition, no other calling. Also, because the church will have been raptured, these young Jews will become God's primary mouthpieces of salvation to the unsaved. This is further evidence the church will be absent during the tribulation, as there is no mention at all of a "bride witness." These Jewish men will be on fire with a message of redemption and rescue through Jesus, and they will travel the world heralding the gospel.

Their Protection—John records that the 144,000 having the Lamb's name and the name of the Father written on their foreheads (Revelation 14:1). In the ancient Roman Empire, a sealed government document signified three things: (1) the document was secured and protected by the power of Rome, (2) it was the property of Rome, and (3) it was authentic and not a forgery.

As believers, we are sealed by the Holy Spirit until the day of our redemption (Ephesians 1:13-14; 4:30). The 144,000 will also be sealed, which will protect them from the tribulation judgments, the antichrist, and all demonic forces (Revelation 9:4). They will be protected all the way up to and through the second coming of Jesus; we know this because we will see them join him on Mount Zion in Jerusalem at the start of Jesus' millennial reign (14:1). All 144,000 will be there. Not one of them will be missing in action. Not one will die. They are contrasted with the Christian martyrs in Revelation 7:16-17, who will not be protected from the brutal persecution that occurs during the tribulation.

What might the "seal" be on these evangelists? We know they will have the names of God and the Lamb written on their forehead. But this mark is distinctively different from the mark of the beast we see in Revelation 13:16. In the same way that God will mark his own, Satan will counterfeit and mimic this practice by marking his worshippers as well. However, the mark of the beast (Greek *charagma*) refers more to an etching or a tattoo-like insignia, whereas the seal of God (*sphragizo*) speaks of a signet ring pressed into wax (the same word occurs ten times in Revelation chapters 5–6, referring to the wax imprint that seals a scroll). Here, the seal more likely has spiritual significance rather than being a physical mark.[4]

The Two Witnesses (Revelation 11:3-14)

There is yet another way people will hear the gospel during this time. God will commission two special vessels for service during the tribulation. He will call them "my two witnesses," and he will empower them with "authority" for their end-times task (Revelation 11:3). "Witnesses" is the Greek word *marturus*, for which we get our English word *martyr*. In the New Testament, it always refers to real people. So these two men are not symbolic, but real. Let's find out more about this divinely empowered dynamic duo.

First, why are there two witnesses? Why not five? Ten? Or 200? In the Old Testament, God required the testimony of two people to confirm a fact or to certify a truth.[5]

And based on the Scripture text, there are strong Jewish overtones to their identities and mission. During the tribulation, God's program on earth is clearly *Jewish*, for he is turning his attention back to national Israel (Romans 11:25-26). This indicates God's purpose and distinction for the nation of Israel and his plan for her preservation, salvation, and ultimately, restoration (Romans 9–11).

What will the two witnesses do? "They will prophesy" (Revelation 11:3). About what? Undoubtedly, judgment and Jesus.

John also records that they will possess the power to "shut up the sky, so that rain will not fall during the days of their prophesying" (Revelation 11:6). They will also be able to destroy those who seek to harm them via fire proceeding from their mouths (verse 5). And finally, they will have the power to turn water to blood, and "to strike the earth with every plague, as often as they desire" (verse 6). They will also be supernaturally protected. And by the way, so are you. You are invincible until your ministry is finished and God says it's time for you to go (Psalm 31:15).

What about the length of their ministry? The Bible makes it plain that they will prophesy for 1,260 days, or one-half of the seven-year tribulation (Revelation 11:3).

What will they wear? Scripture says they will be "clothed in sackcloth" (Revelation 11:3), a burlap-like material that was worn in times of mourning, grief, distress, and seriousness.

What about their identity? They are described as "the two *olive trees* and the two *lampstands* that stand before the Lord of the earth" (Revelation 11:4). This appears to be an allusion to Zechariah 4:1-14 and the ministries of Joshua and Zerubbabel. Joshua was a religious high priest and Zerubbabel was a political leader. Zechariah had a vision of two light bearers or witnesses. Olive oil was used to fuel lamps and was a symbol of the Holy Spirit's anointing, while lampstands were a symbol of light. These two men, Joshua and Zerubbabel, helped to provide leadership during the rebuilding of the temple. And the key to their success is found in Zechariah 4:6: "'Not by might nor by power, but by My Spirit,' says the LORD of hosts."

These two last-days witnesses will be a shining light for Israel, and they may also play some part in the rebuilding of the temple, or at least in the encouragement of those who take part in it.

Do we know their names? Possibly. There are three potential identities of these two mighty men.

1. They will be two prophets who are previously unknown and are raised up in the last days, just like the 144,000.

2. They are Elijah and Enoch, the only two men in Scripture who never tasted death. Elijah went to heaven in a chariot of fire (2 Kings 2:1-12), and Enoch was raptured (Genesis 5:21-23; Hebrews 11:5).

3. They are Moses and Elijah. This is the view I take, for the following reasons:

   • Like Elijah, the two witnesses will call down fire and stop rain (1 Kings 17:1; 2 Kings 1:10, 12; Luke 4:25; James 5:17). Also, the length of the drought (three-and-a-half years) is the same.

- Moses turned the Nile into blood (Exodus 7:17-21) and brought other plagues as well (Exodus 7–11). So will the two witnesses.

- The Old Testament and Jewish traditions expected Moses and Elijah to return in the future. Malachi 4:5-6 says that Elijah will be sent "before the great and terrible day of the LORD." Jesus affirmed this in Matthew 11:14 and Luke 1:17.

- Moses and Elijah represented the whole of the Old Testament—the *law* and the *prophets* (Matthew 5:17; Luke 24:27; John 1:45).

- Both appeared at Jesus' transfiguration (Matthew 17:3).

- Both exited this world in mysterious, unusual ways: Elijah was taken up in a chariot of fire (2 Kings 2:11-12), and Moses was secretly buried by God in an unknown location (Deuteronomy 34:5-6). Jude 9 says the archangel Michael argued with the devil about the body of Moses. This passage appears just before a prophecy concerning the second coming of Jesus.

Further, perhaps no two individuals would be more welcomed and well received by Jewish people who are returning to their roots than these two Old Testament legends. Because of this, it seems plausible to conclude that their ministry will be primarily to, if not exclusively for, the Jews.

For these reasons, I see the two witnesses as likely being Moses and Elijah. By the way, Satan will mimic the two witnesses with two of his own—the antichrist and the false prophet.

When will their ministry take place? It seems most likely that the two witnesses will carry out their task during the first half of the tribulation, for they will be killed at the end of their appointed time of ministry and their bodies will lie in the streets for three-and-a-half days. This timeline is troublesome if they are killed at the end of the second half of the tribulation. For this reason, it makes more sense to place their ministry from the start of the tribulation to the halfway point, when the antichrist assumes full power of the world and unleashes his wrath on the Jewish people (Revelation 12:12-17). His final expression of fury against Israel may very well begin with the martyrdom of the two witnesses.

Where will they die? Presumably in Jerusalem. When they finish their time of testimony, the beast will be allowed to kill them (Revelation 11:7-10). The beast is the antichrist and is the one who will rise from the abyss (verse 7). The dead bodies of the two witnesses will remain in the streets of Jerusalem (symbolically here called "Sodom and Egypt" because it will become like those places). We know they will die in Jerusalem because verse 8 tells us it's "where also their Lord was crucified." It is also worth noting that Jesus Christ is called "their *Lord*." This is a clear apologetic prophecy to Jews and Israel today, proclaiming that nothing could be more "Jewish" than to bow before Yeshua Hamashiach—Jesus the Messiah.

How will they be killed? We are not told, but the beast will finally be allowed to murder them (verse 7). However, their bodies will lie exposed in Jerusalem for three-and-a-half days. In ancient times, to leave dead bodies in the open was to dishonor and discredit those people. Revelation 11:10 says that "those who dwell on the earth" will revel in this moment.

Amazingly, people will even send gifts to one another to commemorate this day (verse 10). No doubt they will dance and party in the streets. It's "Happy Dead Preachers Day!" This illustrates the fact that a righteous prophet is always a torment to an evil generation.

Then, after three-and-a-half days, something unexpected will happen.

The "breath of life from God" will miraculously enter them (verse 11).[6] Then they will stand on their feet, and "great fear" will fall upon those who are watching them. Thousands will be filled with dread, no doubt wondering, *Are they returning from the dead to preach more? Will they now bring more terrible judgments upon us?*

Then a loud voice from heaven will be heard by all: "Come up here" (verse 12). The voice will probably be that of Jesus himself, as John heard the same command given to him in Revelation 4:1. This is yet further biblical evidence that Jesus is the Messiah and Lord of these two Jewish prophets.

As the two witnesses rise up into a cloud, their enemies will watch in stark disbelief and horror. And if one of these men is indeed Elijah, this will be his second supernatural ride from Earth to heaven.

But God won't be finished yet. Their rapture will be accompanied by a great earthquake (verse 13), and one-tenth of the city of Jerusalem will crumble, with 7,000 people killed instantly. Interestingly, a 2013 report from Israel's home front minister said the country must prepare itself for a major earthquake that scientists warn could happen soon. The region has a history of earthquakes, and the last serious one hit in 1927. The report stated that a major earthquake hits the area every 100 years. And the number they predict will die in such a quake? "7000."[7] The phrase translated "people" in Revelation 11:13 literally means "the names of men." It is an unusual expression that some Bible commentators suggest could refer to prominent people in the city, or perhaps even those in the antichrist's administration.

The rest of the people will be "terrified and [give] glory to the God of heaven" (verse 13). The phrase "[give] glory to God" is typically a reference to salvation (Revelation 4:9; 14:7; 16:9; 19:7; see also Luke 17:18-19; Romans 4:20). The fear and glory mentioned here is a strong allusion to genuine repentance, most likely from the Jews living in Jerusalem at this time. During the tribulation, God will reach out to the Hebrew people through the two witnesses in order to draw them to himself.

The Gospel Angel

Another way God will extend his grace during the tribulation is through angelic voices and appearances. Note the progression we've seen as the seven-year tribulation wears on. There is an increasingly supernatural progression to the way the offer of grace is given.

The first people who become saved after the rapture will do so out of a personal realization for what has happened, and they will likely possess a knowledge of the gospel from previous exposure to the truth. Then there will be the preaching of the 144,000 throughout the earth. Alongside that will come the miraculous ministry of the two witnesses, which will conclude with their supernatural resurrection and subsequent judgment on Jerusalem. Now we are introduced to a mighty angel with a "loud voice" (Revelation 14: 7). God's offer of salvation is not going out with a whimper, but rather, with increasing intensity!

Angels carry out a variety of ministries for God and play major roles in end-times events (Matthew 13:41-42, 49-50; 24:31; 25:31; 2 Thessalonians 1:7; Revelation 19:14). They will assist in pouring out God's wrath (Revelation 8:6; 11:15; 16:1). In fact, we see them mentioned in every chapter of Revelation from 4 to 12.

The three angels in Revelation 14 are not necessarily presented in chronological order. Rather, they address issues that span the tribulation and anticipate the judgments of the seventh trumpet (11:15), the bowl judgments (15–16), and the destruction of antichrist's kingdom (18).

The first angel will fly "in midheaven," meaning at "high noon," or directly above the earth (8:13; 19:17). In other words, he will be visible to everyone on the planet.

Some believe that by this time, the spiritual battle between angels and demons will be over (Daniel 10:12-13; Revelation 12:9-12) to the extent that this preaching angel is unreachable and untouchable by the antichrist or demons. Whether he is stationary in the sky and supernaturally heard by everyone or he preaches the gospel while circling the globe at supersonic speeds is not known. What is clear is that he will be heard by "every nation and tribe and tongue and people" (Revelation 14:6).

What message will this angel proclaim? An "eternal gospel." The good news here includes the fact that God is about to deal with the world in righteousness and establish his sovereignty. This angel's mission signifies that this is a "last call" for salvation. And his message is presented as a three-point sermon:

1. "Fear God"—Thus far, humanity has not feared God. And people will get worse and worse from here onward (9:6, 20-21; 16:9, 11, 21).

   Recently, I saw a picture of a woman at a pro-choice rally holding a sign that read, "Mary should've aborted." Another video showed a protestor who snatched a young man's Bible out of his hand and began kicking it across the ground, ultimately hurling it inside a porta-potty into excrement. That is blatant blasphemy. Today, there is hardly any fear of God anywhere (Psalm 36:1; Romans 3:10-18). But during the tribulation, it's going to get much worse.

   This angel heralds a warning to fear *God*, not the tyrannical world leader known as the beast. As believers, we should never fear people, culture, rulers, or nations. As Jesus said in Matthew 10:28, "Do not fear those who kill the body but are unable to kill the soul; but rather fear Him who is able to destroy both soul and body in hell."

This gospel-preaching angel probably won't appear until the seal and trumpet judgments have concluded. Most people will have already rejected the gospel by this point in the tribulation. And yet, he will preach.

His message will be addressed to "those who live on the earth" (Revelation 14:6), a phrase we've seen throughout Revelation, which refers to masses of unbelievers. Because this angel's message will be addressed to "every nation and tribe and tongue and people," it will reach the entire planet (verse 6). This will fulfill Christ's prophecy in Matthew 24:14: "This gospel of the kingdom shall be preached in the whole world as a testimony to all the nations, and then the end will come."

2. "Give Him glory"—This is the angel's second exhortation (Revelation 14:7). In other words, submit and surrender to God. A refusal to do this is at the core of man's prideful rebellion (Romans 1:21).

And why give God glory? "Because the hour of his *judgment* has come." The bowl judgments are coming. Armageddon is coming. Jesus is coming. The great white throne judgment is coming. So turn to God right now!

This is the first occurrence of the Greek word *krisis* ("judgment") in Revelation. But it won't be the last (16:7; 18:10; 19:2). The word carries with it the idea of a decisive judgment that determines a person's future, like a judge handing down a sentence.

Up to this point, the term "wrath" has been used to describe God's judgment. In the remaining chapters of Revelation, the two terms are used interchangeably (14:10, 19; 15:1, 7; 16:1, 19).

3. "Worship Him who made the heaven and the earth"— This is the angel's final call (Revelation 14:7). Of all the possible descriptions of God that the angel is instructed to use, the one he is given depicts God as *creator*. This is the best and most foundational way to understand God (Romans 1:18-22). If you can persuade people that God is not the creator, then you have undermined an essential expression of himself and his relationship to mankind.

When Paul witnessed to the common people, he began by talking to them about God the creator (Acts 14:14-17). And when he spoke to sophisticated philosophers, he did the same (Acts 17:22-31), beginning with the ABCs of God. His approach was different when he spoke to religious people (Acts 17:1-3). Pointing to God as creator is how many of today's people must be introduced to God, as culture has stripped him of his role as the maker of heaven, earth, and humanity. It is no mere coincidence that Satan has long attacked God as creator, wanting to undermine the declaration in Genesis 1:1 that God is the beginner of all things.

The good news this angel delivers is that, even at this late hour, there is still time for people to become saved. The door to the ark is still open. And this is the same good news we ought to proclaim to people today.

The "Bad News Babylon" Angel (14:8)

A second angel will follow the first and will announce the fall of

Babylon, which represents the political, economic, and religious kingdom of the antichrist. Revelation 14:8 marks the first time the word *Babylon* appears in the book. Mentioned almost 300 times in Scripture, Babylon is pictured as a literal city in virtually every instance.

This angel's prophecy concerns the fall of "Babylon the great." This phrase is first seen in Daniel 4:30, and is repeated in Revelation 14:8; 16:19; 17:5; 18:2, 10 (here called the "strong city"), and 21.

Babylon serves as both the antichrist's city headquarters and the symbol of his entire regime, similar to how people in the US would say Washington is both a city and a political administration.

Babylon has always signified evil and rebellion against God. The city was founded by Nimrod (see Genesis 10:9), a proud God-rejecting rebel. Babel was also the first site of an idolatrous religion, and its famous tower was an expression of global rejection of God (Genesis 11:5-9). In the Babylonian language, the word *babel* means "the gateway to the gods." However, in Hebrew, it means "confusion."

In Revelation 17:5, Babylon is portrayed as a harlot, which not only refers to its religious nature but also the way it seduces the world's nations with the "wine of the passion of her immorality" (Revelation 18:3).[8]

The imagery here is that the antichrist has seduced the world with a cup of wine, causing her to be drunk with immorality and allegiance to Satan. The irony here is a play on words—that God will force the antichrist and all those in his kingdom to drink his own cup of wine, one that is filled with wrath (Revelation 14:10; 16:19; 18:6).

From the halfway point of the tribulation onward, the antichrist will not allow people to worship anyone other than himself. But as mighty as his global empire is, at the end of the tribulation, it will fall in one hour (Revelation 18:10).

The angel's message is clear to "those who dwell on the earth." Don't bet on a doomed kingdom, and don't book passage on a ship that God has promised to sink.

The "No Turning Back" Angel (14:9-11)

This is truly God's last call, as history is about to hit closing time.

This third angel warns the people on earth—again with a "loud voice"—telling them there is a line God has determined: Once it is crossed, there is no turning back, no repentance, and no salvation allowed. That point of no return is when a person receives the mark of the beast, indicating their worship of the antichrist (Revelation 14:9). Once this happens, a person's eternal destiny is officially sealed. They are 100 percent guaranteed to feel the full fury of God's wrath and anger toward sin and be tormented 24/7 for all eternity, without so much as one second of relief or rest.

Can you conceive of a worse fate? For those who are alive at this time, this will be their last chance.

There will be no more offers of salvation after this angel finishes his message. This is both a time-sensitive message and a terrifying warning of judgment. And it is inconceivable that anyone would refuse it. However, sadly, most will.

It is here that we must be perfectly clear regarding two undeniable truths: (1) Every person who receives the mark of the antichrist will spend eternity in hell—no exceptions (Revelation 14:9-11; 20:11-15). And (2) no true believer in Jesus can or will receive the mark of the beast (20:4).

It is not clear how long these three angels will preach from the heavens. Theirs may be a one-time appeal, or their proclamations could last well into the second half of the tribulation. But one thing is certain: Satan, the antichrist, and the false prophet will aggressively advance their agenda of 666 and the worship of the antichrist beginning at the midpoint of the tribulation. And we know that the whole earth will worship the beast at this time (13:3-4, 8, 12, 15, 16-17). Therefore, whether the angels carry out their mission for a single day or for short season, this is the last call.

3. The Means of Salvation

Finally, it is also important to know how a person becomes saved during the tribulation. It's simple—it is the same way people were saved during the church age and during the Old Testament dispensation. God has always based salvation on the shed blood of his provision, whom we know to be the Lord Jesus Christ. Even in the Old Testament, people looked *forward* by faith to the Messiah's sacrifice to cover their sin once and for all. Today, we look *back* at his sacrifice, trusting in God's provision through him. Jesus said, "I am the way, and the truth, and the life; no one comes to the Father but through Me" (John 14:6). The same Jesus who saves now will save during the tribulation, redeeming all those who place their faith in him.

Amazing Grace

Can you see now the great grace of our Lord, even during a time of great judgment? Do you see his great patience? (2 Peter 3:9). Even when people dismiss his existence and truth? Even though they don't deserve a second opportunity of salvation during the tribulation? This is how wonderfully merciful our God is.

Yes, there is a coming end-times revival. It will occur primarily during the first half of the seven years of judgments, and God will use every means at his disposal—media, men, messages, miracles, and angelic messengers—to give humanity one final opportunity to escape hell and be declared righteous in his sight.

Today, we are living in the age of grace—a time in which it is much easier to come to Christ than it will be during the tribulation. Even so, God will still reap a harvest of souls in that day. And every person saved will be "to the praise of the glory of his grace" (Ephesians 1:6).

Following the rapture, God's redemptive work will continue unabated. He will be as active as ever, calling people into his kingdom. The book of Revelation affirms these truths about what God will do:

- People will be saved during the tribulation.
- Many people will be saved. There will be a global last day's revival. This is amazing considering that the vast majority of the people on the planet will reject, hate, and blaspheme God (Revelation 9:20-21; 16:9; see also 2 Thessalonians 2:10-12).
- Those who do come to Christ will likely die for their faith shortly after their conversion.
- During the worst of times, God will find ways to save the lost and exalt his grace and mercy.

The fact that people will be saved even in a time of great rebellion against him demonstrates that his grace is greater than any of us ever imagined it to be. Like the hymn says, it's a "grace that is greater than all our sin."[9]

CHAPTER 9

THE KING FINALLY RETURNS

The God Who Is *Faithful*

Revelation 19:1-21

Armageddon.

The word has become synonymous with the end of the world. It represents the apex of the apocalypse. The preeminent showdown between good and evil. Whenever someone wants to use the ultimate hyperbole concerning mankind's extinction, they summon this word. Even so, few actually know what will take place during the real Armageddon, which some have called "the mother of all wars." This includes the fact that what has popularly been thought of as a single battle is actually more of a military *campaign*.

This series of events will be the culmination of seven years of divine judgments from God upon the earth and its inhabitants. It's likely that more people will have died during this period than during all previous conflicts and wars combined. From a human perspective, this bloody epitaph in history is inevitable, as mankind could never achieve lasting world peace on its own. Even secular scientists believe we're near the end. The Bulletin of the Atomic Scientists is known for determining how close they think we are to a global extinction event. Just last year, they set their doomsday clock at 100 seconds to midnight. It's the closest to the "end" they've ever set the clock.[1]

Truth be known, if Jesus Christ did not return, humanity would indeed eventually annihilate itself completely (Matthew 24:22).

The word *Armageddon* means "Mount of Megiddo" and points to a geographical location approximately 60 miles north of Jerusalem that is spread out over 20,000 square miles. This area was the location of some Old Testament battles (Judges 4; 7). Napoleon Bonaparte once visited this valley, remarking, "All the armies of the world could maneuver their forces on this vast plain."[2] Unknowingly, he was prophetically correct.

Among Bible scholars and prophecy experts, there is some debate as to the precise order of this end-times campaign. However, based on what we can know from Scripture, the following is a proposed sequence of events:[3]

1. At the sixth bowl judgment, the Euphrates River will dry up, making it possible for the kings from the East to cross (Revelation 16:12).

2. Three demons performing supernatural signs will lure the antichrist's allies to Israel. Their purpose is to aid the beast in exterminating the Jews once and for all (Revelation 16:12-16). However, Scripture unveils the real reason for their gathering: It's "for the war of the great day of God, the Almighty" (Revelation 16:14). There is biblical evidence supporting the idea that these forces are aware that they are about to go to war with God (Psalm 2:2-3; Revelation 19:19). Imagine how blind, deluded,

arrogant, and demonized they would have to be to do this.

3. Jerusalem will be attacked and fall (Zechariah 12:1-3; 14:2).

4. The antichrist will turn his attention to the south, toward the Jewish remnant hiding in or near Petra, which is in present-day Jordan (Isaiah 34:-7; 63:1-5; Joel 3:19; Matthew 24:15-31; Revelation 12:6,14). Since Jesus previously warned the Jewish people to flee to the mountains (Matthew 24:16), many see the ideal place of refuge as being near Bozrah or Petra, located about 80 miles south of Jerusalem (see Micah 2:12-13; Daniel 11:41; Isaiah 63:1-3).

It is believed this mountainous region, which contains hundreds of clefts and caves, could protectively shelter around a million people. Up to one-third of the Jews will have been hiding there since the midpoint of the tribulation, when the abomination of desolation took place (Daniel 9:27; Matthew 24:15; 2 Thessalonians 2:4). This remnant will be divinely protected by God for three-and-a-half years (Revelation 12:13-17). The other two-thirds of the Jews will be "cut off and perish," presumably slaughtered in an invasion of Israel and Jerusalem (Zechariah 13:8).

5. Israel's remnant will call on the Messiah (Hosea 6:1-3; Joel 2:32; Isaiah 64:1-6; Romans 11:5-27). Ron Rhodes writes, "The antichrist will be impotent and powerless in the face of the true Christ. All the forces of the antichrist will also be destroyed from Bozrah all the way back to

Jerusalem (Joel 3:12-13; Zechariah 14:12-15; Revelation 14:19-20). What a wondrous day that will be."[4]

6. Jesus will arrive at Armageddon to do battle with his enemies (Revelation 19:11-21).

7. Christ will return victoriously to the Mount of Olives (Zechariah 14:4). No one on earth except John has seen *this* Christ for 2,000 years. He will return "with power and great glory" (Matthew 24:27-30). His feet will touch the Mount of Olives, splitting it in two and allowing survivors in Jerusalem to flee (Zechariah 14:4-5; cf. Matthew 24:3; Acts 1:10-11).[5]

In 2004, NBC News reported that a three-year study by the Geological Survey of Israel confirmed this exact area to be at imminent risk for an earthquake, having detected a major fault line running— you guessed it—*right through the Mount of Olives*, east to west. Just another coincidence? Or solid *evidence* that the Bible knows what it's talking about?

Despite three series of horrific judgments, the hearts of men will remain largely unchanged. And Earth's final response toward God? Humanity's last stand? They will assemble in an attempt to thwart God's prophetic plan and Jesus' prophesied reign over the earth. By the time we reach Revelation 19:19, "those who dwell on the earth" are still hating God. Still blaspheming him. Still taunting heaven. Still refusing to repent and believe.

Psalm 2:1-6 best captures their spirit:

Why do the nations rage?
and the peoples plot in vain?
The kings of the earth set themselves,
and the rulers take counsel together,
against the LORD and against his Anointed, saying,

"Let us burst their bonds apart
and cast away their cords from us."

He who sits in the heavens laughs;
the Lord holds them in derision.
Then he will speak to them in his wrath,
and terrify them in his fury, saying,
"As for me, I have set My King
On Zion, my holy hill" (ESV).

The Second Coming (Revelation 19:11-21)

Now let's look at the second coming of Jesus Christ as described in Revelation 19, pausing along the way to examine each aspect of his glorious appearing.

His Arrival (19:11)

There are several words in the New Testament used to describe Jesus' return to our world. One of them is the Greek word *parousia*, meaning "arrival, presence, or coming." It is used 24 times in the New Testament, and 17 of those refer to Christ's future return. Out of those 17, 10 instances are about the rapture, and 7 are about the second coming. It can be argued that the *parousia* occurs in two phases: In the first, Jesus comes *for* his bride, and in the second, he returns *with* her. One is imminent and sign-less, while the other is preceded by 7 years of tribulation and *many* signs. Some people confuse the rapture with the second coming, blending the two into one event, when they are separated by at least 7 years' time.

In Revelation 4:1, heaven opened to let John *in*. But here in Revelation 19:11, heaven opens to let Jesus *out*. This is *the* climactic moment of end-times prophecy, the crescendo of all history. It's *the* most dramatic moment of all time.

Christ will arrive unannounced, uninvited, unwelcomed, and as promised, "like a thief" (Revelation 16:15). And he will receive the kingdom promised to him by his Father (Revelation 5:1-7).

His Transportation (19:11)

Jesus will ride, or glide, to earth on a white horse—a champion steed. In ancient Rome, following a conquest, generals would ride a white horse of victory through the city. The Lord will do the same upon his arrival in Israel, having traded in a humble donkey for a majestic stallion. He will be mounted upon a war horse and land upon the very soil he spoke into existence thousands of years earlier.

His Character (19:11)

Here, Jesus is called "Faithful and True" (Revelation 19:11). Revelation began with a similar description of him (1:5-8). And he is known by the same name to his church (3:14). This is who he is—the true One. Contrast this with Satan's lies (12:9) and the antichrist's evil empire, in which he will constantly lie and deceive the nations (18:23).

But Jesus can be trusted. He is the promise-keeping Christ (John 14:1-3; Revelation 22:7, 12, 20). And he will come back, just like he said he would (Matthew 24:29-31, 36-39, 42-44).

His Judgment (19:11)

Jesus will not come to offer salvation as he did in his first advent. He will not return to teach, perform miracles, heal the sick, feed thousands, attend weddings, hold children in his lap, or tell stories. No, instead he will come to judge and wage war (Revelation 19:11). And it will be a *righteous* declaration of war. There will be no negotiations. No terms of peace. No cease-fires. No white flags. No opportunity for surrender. And there will be no mercy, either. Rather, Christ's righteousness will demand that he judges the world swiftly and decisively, just as he did in the days of Noah (Genesis 6:3-6, 13; 7:23).

And there will be no prisoners of war in this battle scenario, as none of his enemies will survive.

His Appearance (19:12-13)

As in John's vision in Revelation 1:14, the glorified Jesus has eyes that "are a flame of fire" (19:12)—they are penetrating, piercing, and all-seeing (Hebrews 4:13). The eyes that once wept over Jerusalem and shed tears of sorrow at Lazarus' grave will be ablaze with burning wrath.

His head is crowned with many crowns (19:12). This may signify that he has collected all the crowns of the kings of earth, demonstrating his sovereignty over all of them (Isaiah 40:15-25). When David defeated the Ammonites in 2 Samuel 12:30, the king's crown was taken and placed upon David's head.

That Christ would have many crowns is part of what was previewed in Revelation 11:15: "The kingdom of the world has become the kingdom of our Lord and of His Christ; and He will reign forever and ever." Jesus will have rightfully transitioned from a crown of thorns (symbolic of bearing sin) to crowns of glory (symbolic of dominance and sovereignty).

His Secret Name (19:12)

No one will know this secret name "except Himself" (Revelation 19:12). Perhaps there will be a new depth of meaning to his known name, or he will be given a new name or title altogether.

His Garment (19:13)

Jesus will wear "a robe dipped in blood." Some see this as a reminder of his blood shed on the cross. But it is more likely the blood of his enemies. Isaiah 63:1-6 declares,

> Who is this who comes from Edom,
> with garments of glowing colors from Bozrah,

this One who is majestic in His apparel,
marching in the greatness of His strength?
"It is I who speak in righteousness, mighty to save."
Why is Your apparel red,
and Your garments like the one who treads in the wine press?
"I have trodden the wine trough alone,
and from the peoples there was no man with Me.
I also trod them in My anger
and trampled them in My wrath;
and their lifeblood is sprinkled on My garments,
and I stained all My raiment.
"For the day of vengeance was in My heart,
and My year of redemption has come.
"I looked, and there was no one to help,
and I was astonished and there was no one to uphold;
so My own arm brought salvation to Me,
and My wrath upheld Me.
"I trod down the peoples in My anger
and made them drunk in My wrath,
and I poured out their lifeblood on the earth."

So the blood on Christ's robe as he arrives at Armageddon could be from the slaughter of antichrist's army, which had earlier raced to Bozrah in order to destroy the Jewish remnant hiding there (Matthew 24:16-28).

His Revealed Name (19:13)

Jesus is called "the Word" (John 1:1, 14; 1 John 1:1). He is called the Word (Greek *logos*) of God because he is the revelation and full expression of the Father—he is the "radiance of his glory and the exact representation of his nature" (Hebrews 1:3). In John 1:18, we are told he has "explained" the Father. In Colossians 1:15, we read that he is "the image of the invisible God."

His Armies (19:14)

When Christ returns, he will be followed by "the armies which are in heaven" (Revelation 19:14). Who makes up this army that rides behind him on white horses of their own? According to what we can gather from Scripture, this righteous regiment will include these four groups:

1. The bride, the church (19:7-8, 14)—She is clothed in fine linen, bright and clean. That includes *you*!

2. Those who come to faith and are martyred during the tribulation (7:9, 13-14; 17:14). Also clothed in white robes, they are "called and chosen and faithful" (17:14).

3. The Old Testament saints—those who put their faith in God prior to the cross (Daniel 12:1-2; 1 Thessalonians 3:13; Jude 14).

4. All the angels (Matthew 25:31)—It's as if heaven empties itself of the angelic host for this epic event. Imagine the sky filled with untold millions of horses and riders, like many squadrons of fighter aircraft. Wherever one gazes upward, the armies of heaven will be seen.

All those who join Christ at his return are described as "holy ones" (Zechariah 14:5), and all are said to be "following Him on white horses" (Revelation 19:14).

His Weapon (19:15, 21)

Of all those who descend from heaven, Jesus alone possesses a weapon in this war, and only one. It is the "sharp sword" that proceeds from his mouth. His words are all that is needed to win this battle. Consider all that his spoken words have done through the ages: By his word, the worlds were formed (Genesis 1:3; John 1:1-3).

With only a word from his mouth he healed the sick, raised the dead, calmed a storm, cursed a fig tree, and silenced demons, casting them out of people and animals and into the abyss. His word, whether spoken or written, is a powerful, razor-sharp, double-edged sword.[6]

Since Jesus' departure from Earth, his bride has been nourished on this Word, drinking it like milk and consuming it like meat.[7] His supernatural Word is our source of truth and the bedrock upon which we build our lives, relationships, marriages, families, and the church.[8] It is everything the bride needs for life and godliness.[9]

This same Word is impossible to separate from the person of Christ himself. And with it, he will "strike down the nations" (Revelation 19:15). As Jesus descends and looks upon his enemies at Armageddon with his flaming eyes, they will have no chance to launch a counterattack. In the ultimate example of battlefield shock and awe, not a trigger will be pulled nor a shot fired. Instead, Christ's enemies will be annihilated instantly. They will be mercilessly crushed underfoot, like grapes in a winepress.[10]

The slaughter will be so great that we are told the blood from these armies will flow as high as four-and-a-half feet in some places along a 200-mile-long battle line![11] John tells us Christ will tread "the wine press of the *fierce* wrath of God, the Almighty" (verse 15). The outcome will be brutal, bloody, and beyond comprehension (Revelation 14:14, 15-20).

By this time, most of those who remain on the earth will have refused to repent. They will have rejected the preaching of the gospel from the two witnesses, the 144,000, the tribulation Christians, and the angels flying in midheaven. None of these proclamations *from* God's Word will have convinced them to repent. Therefore, Jesus must personally return and destroy them *with* his Word.

This will be the most extensive mass slaughter since the great flood in Noah's day. Jesus will not be some kind of woke social justice warrior or hipster. He won't be a smiling Savior. He will return to wipe the earth clean of Satan and his minions.

His Title (19:16)

On Jesus' bloodstained robe and across his thigh are written "KING OF KINGS, AND LORD OF LORDS." The robe is possibly a banner that is draped across his chest and thigh. This second-coming Jesus is unrivalled in history. He will be undefeated in battle and unforgiving in his last-days judgment.

The risen Christ is the hero of the ages, a conqueror for all time. The world knows virtually nothing about this Jesus described in Revelation. And sadder still is that the church knows very little of this side of Jesus as well.

Today, Jesus Christ is still welcoming repentant sinners. But at Armageddon, he will condemn and kill them all. This is a sobering reminder that God is the One who creates life, gives life, and takes life according to his sovereign desires and purposes (Genesis 6:1-8; Job 14:5; Psalm 90:12; 139:16).

Wherever Christ goes, lives are altered and changed. Consider the "geography of Jesus."

When we go to *calvary*, we see where sin's debt was paid.

When we travel to the *garden tomb*, we see where death's sting was removed.

But for all those who show up at *Armageddon*, a brutal, vengeful execution awaits them at that doomsday location. And the entire planet will witness the carnage (Revelation 1:7).

After this battle, an "angel standing in the sun" will summon all the birds of the air to gather for a great feast, here called "the great supper of God" (19:17-18). They will feast on kings, commanders, and mighty men, gorging themselves on the flesh of the global elites. Those whose careers and egos once soared to meteoric heights will be brought low and humbled before the Jewish carpenter from Galilee.

The antichrist and false prophet will be seized and thrown alive into the lake of fire (19:20-21). These two men who once stood on top of the world and ruled over billions will be reduced to nothing and confined forever as the first-ever residents in God's fiery lake. And the history of mankind will officially end.

Why Is Christ Returning?

In Christ the King's long-anticipated visit back to earth, he will accomplish a host of holy objectives. He will return

➤ to make good on his promise to come back to earth (Zechariah 14:4; Matthew 25:31; Acts 1:9-11).

➤ to defeat his enemies (Revelation 19:19-21).

➤ to redeem and restore national Israel (Isaiah 11:11; 43:5-6; Jeremiah 30:10; 33:6-9; Ezekiel 36:24-38; 37:1-28; Romans 11:25-27).

➤ to judge Gentiles in the sheep and goats judgment (Matthew 25:31-46).

➤ to resurrect Old Testament saints and tribulation martyrs so they can enter the millennial kingdom in their glorified bodies (Revelation 20:4-6; see also Daniel 12:1-4).

➤ to bind Satan for 1,000 years (Revelation 20:1-3).

➤ to begin his millennial reign as King (Isaiah 9:6; Daniel 2:44; Matthew 19:28; Luke 1:32-33; Revelation 19:6).

But the promise of Jesus' second coming is also meant to evoke a response in us right now. Here are some of the ways we benefit from the truths about his return:

➤ We learn the mind and plan of God—that the war at Armageddon will bring a just and righteous judgment against his enemies. Just as was described of those who suffered under the third bowl judgment, "they deserve it"

(Revelation 16:6). This truth should change our minds about how we view God's character and the future.

➤ We see reality and humanity as God does (Romans 1:18-32; 3:10-18, 23; 6:23; Revelation 9:20-2; 16:9-11, 21). This truth should alter our perspective regarding how dark our world is and how desperately people in our generation need salvation.

➤ We get to have front-row seats to the most epic moment in all of history. We will join Jesus in this glorious event and see, from his holy and righteous perspective, all that is happening on earth. And we will participate in and celebrate his victory.

Jesus' second coming will be a visible, violent, decisive, heroic, and regal event! (Revelation 1:7; 19:16). No wonder John couldn't hold back at the end of Revelation, proclaiming, "Even so, come, Lord Jesus!" (22:20 NKJV). The Lord is faithful!

CHAPTER 10

THE LORD'S PRAYER... ANSWERED!

The God Who *Reigns*

Revelation 20:1-10

Walking through my kitchen not long ago, I heard a voice even though no one was around. Now before you wonder if I'm suffering from some sort of mental condition, let me say it was the voice of Alexa, Amazon's virtual assistant technology. But what stunned me wasn't the voice itself, but what Alexa said. She calmly announced, "The millennial kingdom has arrived."

And that stopped me dead in my tracks.

"Alexa," I inquired, "*what* did you just say?" And without missing a beat, she repeated, "The millennial kingdom has arrived."

I must confess, the first thought I had was, *Why would a virtual voice assistant be interested in Bible prophecy?* And the second thought, perhaps on the humorous side, was, *Why was Alexa an amillennialist?*

This puzzled me for a moment until I realized that Alexa often announces when packages arrive at my door. And that's when it hit me. I had ordered a book by Dr. John Walvoord titled—you guessed it—*The Millennial Kingdom*.

Mystery solved.

Understanding the Millennial Kingdom

When it comes to the subject of the millennial kingdom, many questions come to mind:

- What is the millennial kingdom?
- Will there will be a literal 1,000-year millennial kingdom on the earth?
- If so, when will it occur?
- Is it possible it has already occurred?
- Or could it be happening right now?

Great questions.

In the Gospels, Jesus spoke often of the kingdom. The kingdom of God is also mentioned in the Old Testament (Psalms 10:16; 93:1-2; 96:10).

As for the timing of the kingdom, consider these passages: "Repent, for the kingdom of heaven is *at hand*" (Matthew 3:2; 4:17), and "The kingdom of God is within you" (Luke 17:21 KJV).

So is it now, later, or inside me? Which is it?

Scripture makes a distinction between the general sovereignty of God, or the fact that he always rules over the universe, and Jesus' millennial kingdom, whose nature and timing are debated. This chapter is devoted to the topic of Jesus' future kingdom as described in Revelation 20.

Let's begin with the basics. The Latin word *millennium* means "one thousand." The word itself, like many other doctrinal terms we use, is not found in the Bible primarily because the New Testament wasn't written in Latin, but rather, in Greek. So there are no Latin words found in the original manuscripts, nor are there any English words. Words like *trinity*, *inerrancy*, *Christmas*, *Easter*, or even *Bible* don't actually appear in Scripture. However, we do see the truth of the millennium clearly taught.

Three Views of the Millennial Kingdom

In Revelation 20:1-7, we see the number 1,000 repeated six times in seven verses. This repetition is meant to communicate a key aspect regarding Jesus' future kingdom. But what does the number 1,000 mean here? There are three views concerning the 1,000-year-reign of Jesus Christ.

Each of them has to do with the relationship between Jesus' second coming and his reign over all the earth.

Amillennialism

The prefix *a* means "no." Therefore, amillennialism says there is no actual, future, earthly, literal 1,000-year reign of Jesus. Instead, his kingdom exists spiritually in our hearts. The number 1,000 is symbolic and simply refers to an extended period of time. Amillennialism views Satan as being bound at the first coming of Jesus. However, one look at our world quickly dismisses this view, as he is clearly not bound.

Amillennialists do believe Jesus will return one day to judge mankind, but not following the seven-year tribulation that is described in Revelation 6–19. But if Jesus is currently reigning in the hearts of his people, as amillenialists claim, it appears he is doing a poor job. The amillennial view spiritualizes Scripture, interpreting nearly all prophetic passages and numbers in Revelation as *symbolic*. This approach to prophecy was initiated by Augustine and has been the predominant view of the Roman Catholic Church, the Greek Orthodox Church, and many Protestant denominations, including Presbyterians. It was also the view of John Calvin and Martin Luther.

Postmillennialism

This view says Jesus Christ will return to the earth following an undetermined amount of time that includes a golden age of godliness that Christians will usher in through the gospel's global influence upon the world. Postmillennialists see Christianity becoming so prevalent on the earth that Jesus will eventually be welcomed back to end the millennium and inaugurate eternity. Postmillennialism sees the kingdom as *now*, happening and leading to the eventual return of Jesus at his second coming.

However, if it is true that Christians are to bring about God's kingdom to the earth through our worldwide influence, then (1) we can safely conclude that: we are failing miserably, because evil and wickedness are clearly ruling the day. Human society is getting worse, not better. And (2) we have a long way to go before the planet becomes more Christian, because some four billion people still have not yet heard the name of Jesus Christ.

Premillennialism

The premillennial position states that Jesus will return to the earth at his second coming *prior* to establishing a literal 1,000-year reign over the earth. This view sees Christ's millennial reign as occurring in a *future* era, and says that Satan will be bound during this 1,000-year period, according to Revelation 20:1-9.

Premillennialism was the predominant view among the early church fathers: Clement of Rome, Barnabas, Ignatius, Polycarp, Tertullian, and Justin Martyr. Premillennialists believe, as do others who hold to different eschatological views, that God is sovereign and rules over all things at all times, including now (Psalm 115:3). However, the difference is that premillennialism sees a clear distinction between the nature and extent of Jesus' reign in this current age and his rule in the future millennial kingdom. Christ's rule in that day will be global, righteous, and clearly visible.

So Why Premillennialism?

There are several reasons why I believe the premillennial view is the one best supported in Scripture. Keep in mind that how you understand and interpret the 1,000 years in Revelation 20 is determined by how you understand and interpret the rest of Revelation. Like traveling a road leading to a particular destination, your *hermeneutic* (or method of interpretation) will lead you to a particular general understanding of the Bible. In other words, how you begin determines where you end up.

I see the most effective and accurate interpretive method to be the literal, grammatical, historical, cultural, and contextual method. This is how the Bible was meant to be interpreted and understood. And it's how those who hold to the other two views interpret the prophecies concerning Jesus' first coming. Practicing this method, any studious believer can grasp the meaning of Scripture, from Genesis to Revelation—and that includes what it teaches about the millennial kingdom.

With that in mind, here are seven reasons why I believe that Jesus' second coming will precede his establishing of a literal 1,000-year rule upon the earth.

Reason #1—Premillennialism fits well with God's promises made to Abraham and David

In the covenants God made with both men, specific promises were given:

> Abraham was promised that he would be the father of a great nation (Genesis 12:2). That promise was *fulfilled*

literally through the historical growth of Abraham's descendants, who became the Jewish nation.

God promised Abraham he would bless him, and that through him all the nations would be blessed (Genesis 12:3). That promise was also fulfilled literally through Jesus and his sacrifice on the cross.

Abraham and his seed were given a specific area of land (Genesis 12:1; 15:18-21). King Solomon came close to enjoying the fulfillment of this prophecy, but he never ruled over the total land area God promised to Abraham.[1] In fact, Israel has yet to rule over these promised land boundaries. Therefore, this prophecy awaits its fulfillment at a future date. And it will come to pass during the millennial kingdom.

God told David that his "descendant" would reign on his throne forever (2 Samuel 7:12-16). God said "forever" three times in this passage, emphasizing the literal reality of the promise. This prophecy, concerning Christ in Matthew 19:28, Luke 1:31-33, and Acts 1:6-7 has also not yet been fulfilled. Jesus is not currently ruling from David's throne (Hebrews 12:2).[2] At his second coming, however, he will assume his rightful place on this throne (Acts 15:15-18).

Reason #2—Premillennialism harmonizes with the resurrections of Revelation 20:1-6 ("they came to life and reigned with Christ for a thousand years")

The word translated "resurrection" (Greek *anastasis*) is used 41 times in the New Testament and always refers to a literal, bodily resurrection. It does not make sense that tribulation-era saints would be resurrected to reign with Jesus in some sort of symbolic, spiritual kingdom of some undetermined length. Also, why would those unbelievers who died during the tribulation be *physically* resurrected for judgment following a metaphorical 1,000-year period? If the resurrections and judgments are literal, then it follows that the millennium will be as well.

Reason #3—Premillennialism was the dominant view of the early church and remained so for the first 300 years of church history

Here are some of the early church fathers who held this view:

- *Papias* (c. AD 60–130)—the Bishop of Hieropolis, a companion of Polycarp, and a disciple of the apostle John (who wrote Revelation), claimed that the apostles Andrew, Peter, Philip, Thomas, James, John, and Matthew also held to the premillennial position[3]
- *Ignatius* (d. AD 108)—the first-century Bishop of Antioch
- *Polycarp* (AD 69–155)—a disciple of the apostle John
- *Justin Martyr* (c. AD 100–165)—he wrote of Christ's 1,000-year reign in his *Dialogue with Trypho*
- *Irenaeus* (c. AD 130–202)—the Bishop of Lyons, who was also a disciple of Polycarp

It wasn't until Augustine (fourth to fifth century AD) spiritualized the kingdom that the amillennial view gained prominence in the church. Up to this time, the belief in amillennialism was associated with heretical, nonliteral approaches to interpreting Scripture.[4]

Reason #4—Jesus Christ's first coming to Earth was not symbolic or spiritual, but literal

Because the prophecies about Christ's first coming were fulfilled literally, there is no compelling reason to believe the prophecies about his second coming and millennial reign won't also be fulfilled literally, especially since that's what Scripture seems to clearly state (Isaiah 2:3; Daniel 7:14; Zechariah 14:4, 9; Revelation 19:11-21; 20:2, 4).

Reason #5—Premillennialism is upheld by the most plain and natural reading of Revelation's prophecies

We have two options here: Either Jesus' return, future reign on the earth, great white throne judgment, and eternity are literal and real, or they are symbolic, figurative, or take place in an unseen spiritual realm. But there is a problem with interpreting all of Revelation's prophecies as referring to abstract spiritual truths. According to John in Revelation 1:7, at the second coming, "every eye [on Earth] will see Him." Physical eyes will view a physical return. A literal return logically and naturally leads to a physical, literal millennium. Also, Revelation 5:10 says that the saints in heaven will "*reign* upon the earth"—literally.

Reason #6—Premillennialism fits with the binding of Satan

In Revelation 20:1-3, John supplies us with specific details about the binding of Satan. If Satan's shackling were merely metaphorical, it would defeat the whole point of the language John used. Therefore, an actual binding must be in mind here. John, who was inspired by the Holy Spirit as he wrote Scripture, wrote his words carefully. He describes *specific* objects, actions, and places, and even provides a detailed time line: "angel" "key," "abyss," "chain," "hand," "laid hold," "bound," "a thousand years," "threw," "shut it," "sealed it."

The belief that the devil is somehow *currently* bound in what is now said to be Jesus' spiritual 1,000-year reign is untenable. Look around the world. Satan is still very much alive and well on planet Earth. He is still "the god of this world" who has "blinded the minds of the unbelieving" (2 Corinthians 4:4), and he is still "the prince of the power of the air" (Ephesians 2:2). He still "deceives the world" (Revelation 12:9) and acts as our greatest "adversary" (1 Peter 5:8). One thing he is not, however, is "bound."

Reason #7—Premillennialism employs the plain, literal, grammatical approach to interpreting Revelation

It is true that in Revelation, John uses phrases that refer to more general, undefined time periods, such as, "a little while longer" (6:11), "only a short time" (12:12), and "a short time" (20:3). In those instances, God is not specific.

But if the 1,000-year number, repeated 6 times in 7 verses (Revelation 20:1-7), isn't meant to be interpreted literally, then why does God repeat it over and over and over? Why not simply say "a long time"? Why keep repeating a specific number when the Lord could have used other phrases to indicate an unspecified amount of time?

Viewing 1,000 as literal is more consistent with other numbers John portrays as being literal and exact, such as "one hundred and forty-four thousand" (7:4; 14:1), "two witnesses" (11:3), "two hundred million" (9:16), "twelve hundred and sixty days" and "one thousand two hundred and sixty days" (11:3; 12:6), "seven thousand people were killed in the earthquake" (11:13), "ten horns...seven heads" (13:1), "another angel, a third one" (14:9). Why use specific numbers to communicate vague and symbolic concepts? Why didn't God simply say what he meant?[5] And why wouldn't we believe him? To interpret these numbers symbolically only leads to speculation and confusion.

For me, those are seven convincing reasons why the premillennial view best fits with what the Bible teaches about Jesus' second coming and his reign upon the earth.

Having said this, I am not demeaning those who hold to other views. All views should be compared and evaluated against Scripture.

This helps to clears confusion, enables us to be informed, and gives us confidence concerning what we believe.

Both the Old and New Testaments speak of a future, literal kingdom (Isaiah 9:6; Psalm 2:9; Zechariah 14:9). However, only in Revelation do we learn that it's 1,000 years in length.

Specifics About the Millennial Kingdom

Now let's turn our attention to what the Bible says regarding the particulars of this millennial reign on Earth.

Why a Kingdom?

- to give Jesus what is rightfully his (Psalm 2:7-8; Colossians 1:15-16; Hebrews 1:1-2; Revelation 5:1-7)
- to fulfill promises made to Abraham regarding blessing and the land (Genesis 12:2-3; 13:14-15; 15:18-21; 17:7-8; Ezekiel 20:42-44; 36:28-35)
- to fulfill God's promise that the Messiah would reign on David's throne forever (2 Samuel 7:10-17; 1 Chronicles 17:11-14; Isaiah 9:6-7; 11:1)
- to spiritually restore the nation of Israel (Jeremiah 31:31-34)
- to vindicate Jesus' refusal to prematurely accept Satan's offer of the world's kingdoms when he was tempted in the wilderness (Matthew 4:8-10; Luke 4:5-8)

Who Will Be There?

The kingdom will include representatives from every tribe, tongue, people, and nation (Revelation 5:9-10; 7:9) and all saints throughout the ages, including:

- Old Testament saints (Isaiah 26:19; Daniel 12:2)

- martyred tribulation saints (Revelation 6:9-11; 20:4)

- saints who survive the tribulation (Zechariah 12:10; Matthew 25:31-46)—these believers will have mortal bodies, and during the kingdom, they will marry and reproduce (Jeremiah 30:20; Isaiah 66:20; Ezekiel 47:21-23; Zechariah 10:8; Matthew 22:30), and they will enjoy long lifespans (Isaiah 34:24; Ezekiel 34:25-28; Zechariah 14:10-11)

- the bride of Christ (Revelation 19:8, 14)

What Will the Kingdom Be Like?

- Jesus the King will reign righteously over all the earth (Isaiah 9:6-7)

- his throne will be based in Jerusalem (Psalm 2:6-9; Isaiah 2:2-4; Ezekiel 48:30-35; Daniel 7:14; Micah 4:1, 6-8; Zechariah 8:1-3)

- his government will last forever (Isaiah 9:7; Daniel 7:14, 27)

- everyone will know the Lord (Isaiah 11:9; Jeremiah 31:33-34)

- every saint will be fully mature in the Lord (Romans 8:29-30; 1 Corinthians 2:16; 13:12)

- we will worship the Lord in Jerusalem (Ezekiel 40–48; Isaiah 45:23; 52:10; Zephaniah 3:9)

- we will all enjoy eternal life, living with God and knowing him and one another

- we will enjoy global peace (Isaiah 2:4; 9: 4-7), joy (Isaiah 9:3-4), comfort (Isaiah 12:1-2), justice (Isaiah 9:7), and freedom from the curse of sin (Isaiah 11:6-9; 35:9; 65:25)

How Will the Earth Be Different?

Earth's landscape/topography will be radically altered during the tribulation through

- global war (Revelation 6:3-4)
- billions of deaths (6:8; 9:15)
- massive earthquakes (6:12-14; 8:5; 16:18-19)
- the pollution of rivers and oceans (8:8; 16:4)
- devastation from meteors and asteroids (6:13; 8:10)
- one-third of the trees and all green grass will be burned (8:7)
- pollution from war, perhaps nuclear (6:4, 8)
- volcanic eruptions (6:12)

All this will make the earth an undesirable place to live. "Climate change" is indeed coming, complements of Jesus Christ and his wrath.

So what will God do? How will he fix everything? Essentially, he will remake the topography and renew the atmosphere. In Daniel, we read of a 75-day interval between the second coming of Christ and the inauguration of the millennial kingdom. If you recall, the second half of the tribulation will last 1,260 days, but Daniel 12:11 tells us there will be 1,290 days from the midpoint of the tribulation, or the abomination of desolation, and an extra 30 days, presumably to restore the temple for the millennial kingdom. Then, in addition to that, another 45 days will go by before the kingdom officially begins (Daniel 12:12). This is likely when the judgment of the nations (Gentiles) will take place (Matthew 25:31-46).

- Jewish survivors will be judged as well (Matthew 25:1-30)
- the government of the kingdom may also be set up during this 45-day period
- the earth will be ecologically and theologically prepared

These will be among the results of God's extreme makeover of planet Earth:

- the deserts will blossom (Isaiah 35:1-2)
- mountains that were destroyed will presumably be restored, and Jerusalem will rise above the surrounding plain like a jewel (Micah 4:1; Zechariah 14:9-10; Revelation 16:20)
- Jerusalem will be the new world capital (Psalm 2:6; Isaiah 2:3)
- there will be no war nor the devastation associated with it (Isaiah 2:4)
- the planet that has long groaned for redemption will finally exhale with delight (Romans 8:20-22)

Will There Be Animals?

- Yes, but as far as we can tell, not our former pets.
- The curse placed on the animal kingdom because of sin (Genesis 3:14) will be reversed, and there will be no biting or death, or vicious animals (Isaiah 11:6-8; 35:9; 65:25).
- We will enjoy animals and have dominion over them, as Adam did in the garden (Genesis 1:26-28; Psalm 8:3-8; see also Isaiah 11:6-8).
- We might even retain our "flying white horse" from the second coming . We do know that horses will populate the kingdom (Zechariah 14:20).

What Will Our Roles Be?

We will reign with Christ (Daniel 7:18, 22, 27; 2 Timothy 2:12; Revelation 20:4-6). Scripture tells us what this co-reign will look like—we will judge/govern angels (1 Corinthians 6:1-3) and rule over cities (Luke 19:11-26) and nations (Revelation 2:26-28). These responsibilities will be awarded based upon our faithfulness to Jesus, our obedience, and our overcoming tribulation while on earth. We will have unrestricted access to the whole world and enjoy living in God's kingdom.

Will There Be Any Sin in the Kingdom?

Unfortunately, yes. Those saints on earth who survive the tribulation and are still alive at the second coming will enter the kingdom in their mortal bodies. This means they will be able to bear children. These saints and their children will still possess their sin nature, unlike us, and will have the choice to believe in or reject King Jesus. This is the only way to explain the rebellion that will take place at the end of the millennium (Revelation 20:7-9). But keep these points in mind:

- In the kingdom, outward behavior will be kept in check by godly peer pressure.

- Sinful behavior will be greatly curbed by the righteous presence of Christ.

- Sin and disobedience will be addressed swiftly.

Why Will God Free Satan from the Bottomless Pit?

At the close of Christ's 1,000-year reign, Satan "will be released from his prison" (Revelation 20:7). He will immediately begin a campaign of deception on those unbelievers who are alive at this time (verse 8). So what does the Bible tell us about where he has been, and his condition upon his release?

First, consider his prison, called "the abyss" (Revelation 20:3). This place is for the worst of demons (Jude 6; Revelation 9:1-2, 11). Second, whenever Satan is defeated or punished, his anger becomes more intense (Revelation 12:7-9, 12-13). Third, the children and grandchildren who are born to believers and unbelievers during the millennium will possess sin natures. Evidently many of them will end up comprising the "nations" that rebel at the close of the 1,000 years (Isaiah 65:20; Revelation 20:8). From Revelation 20:7-9 we learn these details about the uprising:

- Satan will succeed in deceiving the masses. Nothing will have changed or been rehabilitated in his rotten, evil character.
- He will gather a massive army.
- The war will be very brief, for fire will descend swiftly from heaven and devour everyone.

Then all these enemies will be cast into the lake of fire—forever (20:9-10).

But the nagging question remains: Why will God release Satan? What's the point? Scripture doesn't give a specific answer. But there are several potential reasons:

- to prove the devil's unredeemable nature—he cannot change, even after 1,000 years of solitary confinement
- to demonstrate the inherent wickedness of the human heart (Isaiah 53:6; 64:6; Jeremiah 17:9; Romans 3:10-12; 7:18)
- to show how powerful Satan's deceptive ability is—this power is in effect in our present world
- so God can publicly bring an end to sin and sinners once and for all (Revelation 21:8)

Longing for the Millennial Kingdom

Don't you long for the day when Jesus will make everything as it should be? No more sin, evil, temptation, violence, immorality, murder, injustice, and unrighteousness? That's the kingdom Jesus is coming back to establish—a kingdom you will enjoy as you reign alongside him.

So maybe next time you pray the following prayer, you'll express it with a new depth of longing. In fact, why not pause right now and pray it from the heart?

> Our Father who is in heaven,
> hallowed be Your name.
> Your kingdom come,
> Your will be done,
> on earth as it is in heaven.
> Give us this day our daily bread.
> And forgive us our debts, as we have also forgiven our
> debtors.
> And do not lead us into temptation, but deliver us
> from evil.
> For Yours is the kingdom and the power and the glory
> forever. Amen (Matthew 6:9-13).

CHAPTER 11

THE COURT OF NO APPEALS

The God Who *Recompenses*

Revelation 20:11-15

Following the 1,000-year reign of Christ, God will turn his attention to some unfinished business. To set the scene, Satan is now in the lake of fire. He is gone and will never return to tempt humanity. He will join the antichrist and the false prophet in that fiery hell—they will have already been there for 1,000 years (Revelation 19:20), along with every fallen angel.

What occurs next is perhaps the most terrifying scene in all of Scripture. Revelation 20:11-15 unfolds it for us:

> I saw a great white throne and Him who sat upon it, from whose presence earth and heaven fled away, and no place was found for them. And I saw the dead, the great and the small, standing before the throne, and books were opened;

and another book was opened, which is the book of life; and the dead were judged from the things which were written in the books, according to their deeds. And the sea gave up the dead which were in it, and death and Hades gave up the dead which were in them; and they were judged, every one of them according to their deeds. Then death and Hades were thrown into the lake of fire. This is the second death, the lake of fire. And if anyone's name was not found written in the book of life, he was thrown into the lake of fire.

The King's Court

John's eyes are once again drawn to God's intimidating throne. It is described as being "great" and "white." No doubt this throne is large, but this description also speaks to the absolute authority of its occupant over the universe (Psalm 9:7-8). The same scene is described in Daniel 7:9-10. This is the same sovereign and throne we saw back in Revelation 4:8-11. We know from Revelation 7:10 that salvation comes from him who sits on the throne. We also discover from Revelation 3:21 that Jesus is sitting on that throne, and we know from John 5:22, 26-27 that all judgment has been given to him. Peter echoes this truth in Acts 10:42, referring to Christ as the "Judge of the living and the dead." This truth is repeated several other places in Scripture as well (Acts 17:31; Romans 2:16; 2 Timothy 4:1; Philippians 2:10-11). And it is also the same throne we see in the new heavens and the new earth (Revelation 22:1, 3).

The one who is seated on this throne is so powerfully intimidating that "earth and heaven" will flee at the time of this judgment (Revelation 20:11). Even creation itself will sense the gravity of his righteous presence. According to many scholars, this is likely a reference to God's destruction of the heavens and the earth (2 Peter 3:10-13). Because he created the world and the universe, it therefore stands to reason that he can also *un*create them as well. In the next chapter, we will take a detailed look at what that new heavens and earth will be like.

The scene here in Revelation 20 exposes us to yet another aspect of God's retributive wrath—this one presumably a final expression of it. Though all of God's attributes are in flawless harmony with one another, not all of them are expressed with the same degree at any given time. We see throughout Scripture the manifestation of God's nature—his creative power (Genesis 1:1), his wisdom and knowledge (Jeremiah 17:10; Romans 8:26), and his great compassion (Psalm 51:1; Isaiah 49:13; 54:10; Mark 1:40-41). And all through Revelation, we've seen God's apocalyptic wrath on display for all the world to see. But this is different. And what makes his wrath unique here is the finality of it.

Too Late for Repentance

This arguably is the most dreaded moment of all time. The gravity of this scene cannot be overstated. John is our tour guide describing what he sees, and it is not good. He is confronted by the sight of "the great and the small, standing before the throne" (Revelation 20:12). This throng of humanity will include all the unbelievers who have ever lived—from Adam's era through the days of Noah. From the residents of Sodom and Gomorrah to all those who existed in the ancient kingdoms of Babylon, Assyria, Medo-Persia, Greece, and Rome. From all those people groups who were contemporaries of Israel's past history—the Jebusites, Canaanites, Edomites, and Philistines. Standing among this crowd will be every individual throughout the last 2,000 years who rejected the offer of salvation through Jesus Christ.

With trembling knees, every pagan philosopher, arrogant and ungodly educator, unbiblical religious follower, and self-reliant king and politician will be there. All who took defiant stands against

God and truth will be there—every deluded and depraved soul who embraced the moral lies of the world and proudly rejected God's righteous standards and their need for salvation in Christ. They will be seized with sheer terror as they look upon this great white throne and him who sits upon it.

Many of the world's celebrities and elites will be there—all those who chose to pursue fame and riches and power over surrendering their lives to the creator. Before the throne, they will be nameless and ordinary. Their fame and wealth and power will mean nothing.

Morally upright people, charitable church members, and religious people from all over the world who did not seek Christ as their means of salvation will stand in this crowd. Jews, Muslims, Hindus, Buddhists, atheists, agnostics, theists, and people from every religious and philosophical persuasion will be part of this massive, condemned congregation.

Poor people will be there too, along with the rich. The educated will be standing shoulder to shoulder with the untaught. The Wall Street hedge fund broker next to the West Virginia coal miner. Debutants alongside derelicts. Teenagers together with the elderly. And every person who believed the lie of Satan and voluntarily took the mark of the beast will no doubt stand there with utter self-hatred. But it will be too late. In fact, the very moment people receive the beast's mark and become willing worshippers of the antichrist, their doom is sealed (Revelation 14:9-11). At the great white throne judgment, billions upon billions of people will be resurrected from their confinement in hell to stand before the throne (John 5:29; Acts 24:15).

Noticeably absent here are the redeemed, the chosen, those who are part of the bride of Christ. There is no mention of believers in this scene, nor will they need to be there, for their judgment already took place upon the Lord Jesus Christ at the cross (Romans 8:1;

2 Corinthians 5:21). They will already be enjoying God and all that heaven has to offer.

But this untold number of condemned people will be given a brief relief from their torment in hell in order to be brought into God's courtroom and to appear before his great white throne. Depending on when each of these passed from this life to the next, they will have suffered unimaginable torment for as little as a few days (since being consumed with fire from heaven in the rebellion at the close of the millennial kingdom) to thousands of years (since the first humans died during Adam's day).

This Was Your Life

Some have speculated about whether or not people will be isolated from one another in hell. Scripture doesn't say, but two realities speak to this issue: (1) Hell is portrayed as a place of "outer darkness" (Matthew 25:30). If this is a literal description, then certainly those who are there will experience a separation and loneliness of the soul to which no earthly experience can compare. God is light (1 John 1:5), the absence of a relationship with God would certainly bring a great darkness to the soul, if not actual darkness as well. It's possible these people will be aware of untold billions of others occupying the same hellish place, but even so, this would prove inconsequential and of no comfort to them because (2) the excruciating level of physical pain, emotional terror, and spiritual torment they will be subject to will be so all-consuming that it is unlikely other voices will be understood above the unending, bloodcurdling screams of their own mouths (Luke 16:23-24; 2 Thessalonians 1:9; Revelation 14:10-11; 20:10). And even if they are heard, the echoes of others' shrieks of torment would only add to the agonizing soundtrack of their own insane howls of horror.

What this sea of humanity will share in common is a disdain for

God and a love for self while on earth. Every single one of them, by choice, died without Jesus. And while standing before the great throne, no doubt trembling in terror, their attention will suddenly be diverted to a stack of books.

These heavenly books, hidden for centuries and brought out especially for this day, contain the evidence of indictments before the King of the universe (Revelation 20:12). They are, essentially, Exhibit A for the prosecution (Jeremiah 17:10; Ecclesiastes 12:14; Matthew 12:36-37; Romans 2:9, 16). For those who have been summoned to the grand courtroom, there is no mediator. No court-appointed defense attorney. And no self-defense. The chance for mediation and the right to be represented before the judge of all the earth was forfeited when they departed Earth, having lived their entire lives without trusting in the one who sits on the throne (Matthew 16:27; 1 Timothy 2:5). According to Jesus, there will be "many" who offer a desperate plea (Matthew 7:21-23). Having believed that prophesying in the name of Christ, supposedly casting out demons, and performing "miracles" was a sure sign of salvation and God's favor on their life and ministry, they will discover that none of their incantations and spiritual mind tricks were biblical. They bought into the lies of the prosperity gospel, the "name it and claim it" theology, and the heresy that Christians can access some sort of divine power if they simply speak it or declare it to be so—"in Jesus' name."

But it was all deception founded upon faulty interpretations of Scripture. And Jesus' response to these prosperity preachers, healers, and professing Christians who swallowed this aberrant teaching hook, line, and sinker? He will disavow them, denying that he ever knew them.

A second book will be opened, Exhibit B, here called the "book of life" (Revelation 20:12). This book contains the names of God's elect, chosen "in Him before the foundation of the world" (Ephesians 1:4). These names are indelibly written in eternal ink. They cannot be erased or expunged (Revelation 3:5). They are there by divine decree and sovereign choice, a truth that ultimately, only God can explain.

Presumably, a "recording angel" will open the sacred heavenly books. The deeds contained within are also written with ink that cannot be erased. Scripture doesn't say, but it's possible that each person has his or her own "book"—one consisting of a detailed listing of every deed they ever committed. Because every person's actions are a reflection of their hearts, motives, and minds, those recorded deeds will be an accurate representation of their lives, making them admissible evidence in heaven's high court.

Imagine, from our earthly perspective, the amount of time it would take to process billions of cases before the great white throne. But consider also that time itself will be irrelevant (or perhaps even nonexistent) at this point in eternity. There will be no clocks in the courtroom, no sensation of time. No night or day. No measure of minutes, hours, days, months, or years. Only the moment itself. It is the eternal "now."

Also, consider that God's supernatural knowledge and sovereignty will be able to process these billions of judgments simultaneously—much in the same way that currently, he is able to simultaneously hear and answer the prayers of millions across the globe. The phrase "every one of them" in Revelation 20:13 certainly refers to the extent of this judgment, and is a strong indicator that each person will appear individually before Christ and his throne. Judgment will be a one-on-one encounter, a face-to-face experience with the exalted carpenter from Nazareth.

But whatever the time frame of this event, John simply records that "the dead were judged from the things which were written in the books, *according to their deeds*" (Revelation 20:12). That last phrase indicates that there will be degrees of judgment and punishment in the afterlife (as confirmed by Matthew 11:21-22; Romans 2:6; Hebrews 2:2). We already know that there are degrees of reward in heaven (Matthew 16:27; 19:28-29; 20:1-5; 25:14-30; 1 Corinthians 3:11-15). It makes sense that, though every person who dies without forgiveness through Christ will suffer eternity apart from God, a just God would not punish a morally upright religious person with the same wrath as he will a ritualistic child abuser. Adolf Hitler certainly deserves a greater punishment for facilitating the murder of six million Jews than others who committed much less atrocious sins.

Now, it is true that merely by being born a sinner we have inherited condemnation (John 3:18, 36). In that sense, all humankind is equally sinful. But not so when people are judged "according to their deeds." This is not to say that hell will not be terrifying and awful for those whose deeds are not as heinous as others. All who are judged before the great white throne will suffer incomprehensible pain for eternity.

John records just how comprehensive this judgment is when he says, "The sea gave up the dead which were in it, and death and Hades gave up the dead which were in them; and they were judged, every one of them according to their deeds" (Revelation 20:13). It won't matter how long people will have been dead or how they died. Whether blown up in war, decayed in the grave, or drowned in the sea and consumed by creatures, God knows where everyone's molecules are. Every person's body will be re-created and resurrected from wherever they are while their spirits will be simultaneously retrieved from Hades, where they have been suffering since the moment they departed from their bodies. Body and soul will be reunited to stand before Judge Jesus.

Eternal Anguish and Torment

Today, people march for and demand their "rights" and "justice." However, when they stand before God at this throne of judgment, the only rights that exist will be those that belong to God, and justice will be the *last* thing on anyone's mind. By virtue of the fact that all of them have already spent time in hell suffering for their sins, they will be well aware of their guilt and deserved punishment before a holy God. And standing before the judge of the universe and receiving their final sentence is the last thing they will desire. Even so, this is an unavoidable appointment. They will not be able to resist the divine summons that will draw them out of their soul's torment in hell.

Strangely enough, and even though Scripture doesn't talk about this, it is fair to say that a wide range of emotions will be swirling like a tornado inside the hearts and minds of these condemned souls.

- *Fear* because they are standing before the throne of a holy and righteous God.

- *Dread* because they know what verdict is coming. They know what is inside those books concerning them and their deeds.

- *Regret*, for how can one stand before a majestic and holy God in all of his radiant glory and beauty and not realize how they not only wasted their lives, but also missed a relationship with Jesus and the joy that relationship brings?

- *Hatred* for self and even more so for God because the human heart is "more deceitful than all else and is desperately sick" (Jeremiah 17:9). Their minds and souls will have grown more corrupt and developed more anger against God since being confined to their cell in hell. Like their tribulation-era counterparts, the more God's wrath falls on them, the more they will hate and blaspheme him (Revelation 9:20-21; 16:8-9, 10-11, 14).

In Revelation 20:14, we witness the official end of physical death and Hades as they are both thrown into the lake of fire to be consumed. Bible commentator Robert Thomas observes here how death and Hades are "inseparable companions, two voracious monsters who have swallowed all past generations and now meet the same fate as the prey they have just engorged."[1]

The lake of fire here is called "the second death," physical death being the first. It is this second death that "has no power" over those believers who will be raised at the start of the millennial kingdom (verses 4, 6).

The hearing and trial are now a forgone conclusion. It's time for the sentencing.

After a careful check, all those whose names were "not found written in the book of life" will be "thrown into the lake of fire" (verse 15). This empties the courtroom completely, as 100 percent of those summoned and gathered before the throne will be cast into the flames. And because they will have been restored to their previous physical bodies, their eternal pain won't merely be spiritual, but will be physical as well, according to Jesus (Matthew 10:28). The whole person will be cast into the terrible lake of fire.

Elsewhere, both Jesus and an angel announce that these people's torment will continue for eternity—forever and ever and ever (Matthew 25:41, 46; Revelation 14:11). And the smoke of that fire will rise in the presence of "the holy angels and in the presence of the Lamb" (Revelation 14:10). This tells us several things:

First, despite folklore and movies to the contrary, the devil and his demons are not in charge of hell or of tormenting people there. Rather, God himself will rule over hell and will administer its punishments. The lake of fire will be filled with and fueled by God's wrath, not Satan's.

Second, the lake of fire is eternal, leaving no room for the doctrines of soul sleep, purgatory, an intermediate state of being, universalism (where everyone is saved), annihilation of the wicked (where those who go to hell will cease to exist), or any type of second chance at redemption. No, this is a conscious, everlasting torment in which every occupant will be awake, alert, and on fire with God's hot, furious wrath. And it will never stop. It will never let up or lessen in its intensity. It will be constant, consistent, and all-consuming. There will not be a single second of relief for these Christ-rejecting persons—only a perpetual, persistent pain that pen and ink could never describe, nor human thought ever invent or imagine.

This eternal torment, and its accompanying smoke, will serve as an everlasting reminder to the redeemed in heaven of how holy, righteous, just, and wrathful our God is. In eternity, we will not only praise him for his love and grace, but also for his wrath and retribution upon his enemies (Revelation 6:9-11; 19:2). In the new heaven, we will praise him for *all* his attributes.

This great white throne judgment reveals to us the destiny of those who are condemned. They will be thrown into the lake of fire, a place of darkness (Matthew 8:12; 22:13; 25:30; Jude 1:13), torment (Revelation 14:11), and the weeping and gnashing of teeth (Matthew 13:41-42).

This is the real "sinners in the hands of an angry God."

In summary, the chronology of this judgment appears to be as follows:

1. The sea and Hades will give up their dead bodies (Revelation 20:13).

2. All the unredeemed in hell will be summoned before the throne (verse 13).

3. The old heavens and the earth will be destroyed, disintegrating from the presence of him who sits on the throne (verse 11; 2 Peter 3:10-13).

4. The books documenting people's deeds will be opened (verse 12).

5. The book of life will be opened (verse 12).

6. Every person will be judged by Jesus (verses 12-13).

7. Death and Hades will be thrown into the lake of fire (verse 14).

8. All the condemned will be thrown into the lake of fire (20:15).

Symbolic, Spiritual, or Physical and Literal?

The sobering reality that those who reject God will spend eternity in the lake of fire raises a couple of questions:

1. Is the fire in the lake of fire literal or symbolic?

This lake of fire may already exist, having been previously prepared for the devil and his angels (Matthew 25:41). However, it is presently vacant. Also, one of the New Testament words describing the final hell is *Gehenna*, which referred to a place southwest of Jerusalem known as the Valley of Ben-Hinnom. In the Old Testament, unbelieving Israelites sacrificed their children to demonic gods there (Leviticus 20:2; 2 Kings 23:10; Jeremiah 19:2-6; 32:35). In fact, Jeremiah even called it "the valley of the Slaughter" (Jeremiah 7:32).

During the time of Christ, the same valley served as the garbage dump for Jerusalem. Fires constantly burned there, and the smell was horrible. The place was also infested with maggots, or worms. Jesus used the familiar imagery of Ben-Hinnom to picture what hell would be like (Matthew 5:22, 29, 30; 10:28; 18:9; 23:15, 33; Mark 9:43, 45, 47; Luke 12:5). As we survey the New Testament, we see the word *fire* used to describe those in torment.[2]

But is it a literal fire, a symbolic fire, or something else? Of course, the physical elements that make up fire as we know it are all created by God, so he certainly has the prerogative to use real fire. So if the fire is literal, then the resurrected bodies of the condemned are such that physical fire will burn them but somehow not consume them (Isaiah 66:24; Mark 9:48-49). There are some who reject this idea, believing instead that the term *fire* is simply a metaphor that means "the grave." Other more liberal thinkers and theologians see *hell* as referring to present-day sufferings on earth that we create, not an eternal place of God's wrathful punishment and retribution. This is not supported in Scripture.

However, if the word *fire* does not refer to the literal kind of fire we see and experience here on earth, then it is a symbol of something far worse. A symbol, by definition, points to something even more real than itself. So, if "the lake of fire" is a word picture, it represents a horrific physical location that houses a far greater and more severe torment than literal fire could present.

2. What kind of God would send people into a lake of fire?

This is a fair question, and one that falls into the "I am glad you asked" category. One may quietly counter by responding, "God doesn't send anyone to hell. They send themselves." And Scripture does say that it is people's own "deeds" that seal their sentencing to the hellish lake (20:12-13). However, the Bible also makes it clear that people do not voluntarily walk or jump into this fiery lake, but rather, are "thrown" into it (verse 15). The word used here in the New Testament is the same one used to describe Peter and Andrew as "casting" their fishing net into the water (Matthew 4:18). The word is also used to picture being "thrown" into prison (Matthew 5:25), and to describe physical bodies being "thrown" into the fire of hell (verse 29). In each of those instances, as in Revelation 20, an outside force is acting against the subject. It is assumed that angels will assist Jesus in physically tossing the lost into the lake of fire.

"That's not fair!"

But returning to the original question: What kind of God would do this? A God who...

- is righteous and cannot tolerate sin in his presence (Habakkuk 1:13; Romans 6:23)

- loves mankind, and from the very first sin, set in motion the means for our redemption (Genesis 3:15, 21)

- is merciful, gracious, forgiving, and welcoming of anyone who calls on his name and comes to him (Psalm 145:8-9; John 6:37; Romans 10:13)

- gave his Son as a sacrifice for our sins (John 3:16; Romans 5:8)

- is patient and slow to anger, not willing that any should perish but for all to come to repentance (Psalm 103:8; 2 Peter 3:9)

- created each one of us, allowed us to live in his world, breathe his air, and hear the good news of the gospel

- is a righteous judge filled with fierce wrath toward sin and sinners, and remains in a state of anger toward them until they repent and believe in the Lord Jesus Christ (Psalm 7:11; Romans 5:1; 8:1; Revelation 14:10-11; 15:7)

- pleads with all those who are lost to come to him in faith today while they can still hear his voice (Isaiah 1:18; 45:22; 2 Corinthians 6:2)

You see, we really don't want God to be *just* toward us. And we certainly don't want him to give us what we deserve. What we want is for him to be merciful and gracious, and to accept our humble confession of sin and receive our faith in his Son. However, all those who reject God's open offer of salvation will find themselves standing before the great white throne and discover their destiny to be the lake that burns with fire and the all-consuming wrath of Almighty God.

CHAPTER 12

THERE'S A NEW WORLD COMING

The God Who *Recreates*

Revelation 21:1–22:5

Most likely you have heard the old adage, "You're a sight for sore eyes." First documented in 1738, this saying communicates the joy or relief a person would feel upon seeing someone they're glad to see. It is also used to express gratefulness over seeing someone after going through a hard time. The person becomes a welcome sight in the eyes of the beholder. The phrase isn't used that much anymore, but considering the world we're living in, we could definitely use a "welcome sight" now.

By the time we get to Revelation chapters 21–22, the apostle John has seen some dark and disturbing sights. It began with the shock and trauma of seeing the glorified Christ in chapter 1. John was then catapulted up to heaven, where he gazed upon the throne of the all-sovereign God and witnessed the celestial worship taking place there. In Revelation 5, his eyes filled with tears when no one was found worthy to break the seven-sealed scroll.

From there, John witnessed the apocalyptic judgments of Revelation 6–18, which included global war, famine, billions dying, ecological disasters, cataclysmic disturbances in the heavens, demonic creatures tormenting mankind, the rise and rule of antichrist, the desecration of the Jewish temple, the mark of the beast, and the blaspheming of God by both the antichrist and humanity.

And just as John was catching his breath, the Son of God came down from heaven to earth in glorious victory and slaughtered millions with a sword coming out of his mouth. Following this, John's aged eyes witnessed more end-times judgments, after which his Lord established a 1,000-year reign upon the earth. Evil then raised its ugly head once again as Satan was released from his millennium-long incarceration, whereupon he again deceived millions and stirred up a rebellion against King Jesus. After seeing the insurgents incinerated, John surely wished to close his weary eyes and rest for a while from all the blasphemy and bloodshed.

But it was not to be.

After this massive insurrection was quelled, John found himself a spectator at the great white throne judgment. There, he watched as billions of souls were individually tried, condemned, sentenced, and sent into the lake, which burns with fire and brimstone.

If ever a man needed a vacation, it was John. Surely bracing himself for what might come next, he looked to see an unexpected view, one he may have thought would never come. Revelation 21:1 states, "I saw a new heaven and a new earth; for the first heaven and the first earth passed away, and there is no longer any sea."

This, for John, was truly "a sight for sore eyes."

Old Things Have Passed Away

Ever since Adam's fatal fall in the garden some 7,000 years earlier, the earth, including all of creation, has groaned for redemption (Romans 8:22). But in order to fully purge the universe from sin and all its effects, God will find it necessary to renew everything. And for that to happen, the old earth, including heaven, will require what Bible teacher John MacArthur calls "a major cosmic remodeling."[1]

This will involve the total destruction of the present universe using intense heat. Peter put it this way:

> The present heavens and earth are being reserved for fire, kept for the day of judgment and destruction of ungodly men…But the day of the Lord will come like a thief, in which the heavens will pass away with a roar and the elements will be destroyed with intense heat, and the earth and its works will be burned up (2 Peter 3:7, 10).

God's destruction of all the physical elements in the universe will occur with enormous energy, making a nuclear explosion seem like a firecracker by comparison. This cosmic demolition was planned long ago, as Isaiah prophesied 700 years before Christ:

> Behold, I create new heavens and a new earth;
> and the former things will not be remembered or come to mind.
> But be glad and rejoice forever in what I create;
> for behold, I create Jerusalem for rejoicing
> and her people for gladness.
> I will also rejoice in Jerusalem and be glad in My people;
> and there will no longer be heard in her
> the voice of weeping and the sound of crying (Isaiah 65:17-19).

All the existing atoms, neutrons, protons, and electrons across the entire physical universe will vaporize into nothing, all the way down to the subatomic level. Everything that is will simply cease to exist. In its place, a "new heavens and a new earth" will instantly emerge, created by divine fiat. Once again, the voice command of God is all that will be necessary to speak a new physical world into existence.

The created order, with all its components, has been God's domain from its inception, ever since he originally created it from nothing thousands of years earlier (Genesis 1:1; John 1:1-3; Colossians 1:16). And all this time, it has been his supernatural, invisible power that has held the universe and its atoms together (Colossians 1:17). All that is necessary for the universe to cease to exist is for God to simply stop holding it together (Job 34:14-15). In fact, the word Peter uses to describe this act of destroying literally means "to unleash" or "to unbind" (2 Peter 3:10). Therefore, when God destroys the present universe, what was previously bound by his energy will be *un*bound and blazed into oblivion by a force equal to the energy it originally took to create it.

Both Jesus and the writer of Hebrews affirmed the existence of this future reality (Matthew 5:18; Luke 21:33; Hebrews 1:10-12). What remains when the dust settles will be only those things that last forever—God, his Word, and the spiritual beings he created.

What God will then create is a space that is free from sin and all its residual effects—that is, a completely new heavens and earth.

Everything you and I have ever known in this world has been tainted by decay and death. But a better world is coming. And imagine how much more glorious it will be!

Behold, New Things Have Come

So what does Revelation reveal about this coming new world? John's first words about this new creation describe a "new Jerusalem, coming down out of heaven from God" (Revelation 21:2). The city is portrayed as "a bride" fully prepared and adorned "for her husband." More about this in a moment.

Next, John hears a loud voice coming from God's throne: "Behold, the tabernacle of God is among men, and He will dwell among them, and they shall be His people, and God Himself will be among them" (verse 3). The tabernacle, as we learned earlier, signifies the holy of holies, or the place where God himself is. Nothing here will separate the saints from the closest possible proximity to their God. He will "be among them"! This is perhaps the best definition of heaven given in all of Scripture. And the natural, residual benefits of such an intimacy with God are then listed for us, primarily from the perspective of what *won't* be in heaven. What John catalogs here are mostly the things that made life on earth difficult and miserable.

He begins back in verse 1 by stating that on the new earth, "there is no longer any sea." Though some see this as symbolic of unbelieving humanity, it is best to understand this passage in its plain sense. The topography and geography of the new world will be radically different and much more conducive to humanity. Presently, all life here on planet Earth depends on water to survive. But in the new heavens and the new earth, our bodies won't require water because they will have been made imperishable and immortal—they will be glorified (Roman 8:30; 1 Corinthians 15:53-54). No sea also means there will be no hydrological cycle, and therefore no rain. Even so, water will be plentiful in supply, as there will be a "river of the water of life" for us to enjoy in the new Jerusalem (Revelation 22:1-2).

Here are some of the negatives of our current earthly existence that will not be present in the new world:

No tears (21:4)—There will be nothing in our new life that prompts tears to flow from our eyes.

No death (21:4)—Our ultimate enemy, death, will be forever defeated and driven out of existence by the conquering, risen Christ

(1 Corinthians 15:54-57). As we saw in the previous chapter, death will be thrown into the lake of fire and will remain there for eternity.

No mourning (21:4)—This logically follows from the fact there will be no death. This means there will be no sadness—not even a frown will be seen! There will be no goodbyes and no heartaches that result from being separated from loved ones. Nothing in the new world will ever cause even the slightest bit of sorrow.

No crying (21:4)—We've already seen that tears will be a thing of the past. There also won't be any weeping either. This is in stark contrast to those who will be thrown into the lake of fire, where "there will be [eternal] weeping" (Luke 13:27-28).

No pain (21:4)—The well-worn workout mantra "No pain. No gain" won't apply in the New Jerusalem. There, we will gain *without* pain! Our current life is marked by the threat and reality of physical pain and discomfort. But our new bodies will be reformatted so that we not only feel no pain, but we'll be completely immune to it. Our bodies will be imperishable and therefore impervious to pain (1 Corinthians 15:50, 53-54). The sting of death will have been removed, and along with it the sting of pain.

Romans 6:9 declares concerning Jesus, "Knowing that Christ, having been raised from the dead, is never to die again; death no longer is master over Him." This is an argument from the greater to the lesser. If Christ—and we who are made like him—cannot die, then we also cannot experience pain. There is absolutely no scenario in our future existence that could ever threaten us with pain, hurt, or suffering of any kind! (1 John 3:2). The reason for all this, declares the one on the throne, is "I am making all things new" (Revelation 21:5).

No thirst (21:6)—We will experience a specific kind of thirst in the New Jerusalem, but it won't be as a result of having a parched throat or an empty stomach. Rather, this thirst will arise from a new kind of desire, one that doesn't come from lacking or needing something. Instead, it will stem from a positive desire to enjoy the "water of life" that flows from the very throne of God (22:1). We don't really have a category for or comparison to this concept in our current life. The closest correlation might be the sensation we experience with the first sip of a thirst-quenching, delicious beverage. In the New Jerusalem, we will drink at this free fountain as if we were drinking eternal life itself straight from God. Imagine how satisfying this water will be!

Every one of the above-listed positives will come standard with our "move-in package" as part of the eternal inheritance we receive from our amazing, gracious God (21:7).

But wait—there's more!

No sinners (21:8)—In the New Jerusalem, we will be separated by an impassable gulf from all those whose lives were marked by sin and unbelief while on earth. There will be zero danger from them, and no threat of harm or temptation. Instead, we will be surrounded by saints who love God wholeheartedly like we do.

No temple (21:22)—There will no longer be any need for a physical representation of God's presence, as happened in the Old Testament era and will happen during the millennial kingdom. The Lord and the Lamb will be our temple. We won't need to travel to a geographical location in order to worship God because the presence of the Lord will always be with us (21:3).

No sun, moon, or created light source (21:23-25; 22:5)—It's hard to imagine a light source other than the sun. After all, the sun is all we've known. But the God who "makes all things new" will blow our minds by illuminating our world with his own glory. This will be a different kind of light, one that no man has ever seen nor conceived of. This light will be perfect, and there will be no darkness at all (1 John 1:5).

No closed gates (21:25)—The New Jerusalem does have gates, but they will always remain open. There will be no locks on these gates because there will be no threat of invasion from outsiders. And we will enjoy unlimited access and freedom to come and go as we please. Perhaps we will gather at the gates every now and then to talk to one of the twelve angels stationed at them, or just to meet and fellowship with one another.

In summary, anything here on this earth and in this life that exists because sin entered the world will be noticeably and joyously absent in the next world.

The Big Cube

Next, John turns his attention to the special city, the Father's house, which Jesus has prepared for us. Twice, the New Jerusalem is called the bride of the Lamb (Revelation 21:2, 9). This is not to confuse it with the church, who is also called the bride (19:7) and portrayed that way in the New Testament (John 14:1-3; 2 Corinthians 11:2; Ephesians 5:25-26). Rather, what may be more in mind here—in the context of Revelation—is the contrast between the great prostitute, Babylon, the city of Satan, and the purity and holiness of God's bride and city, Jerusalem.

That this city is an actual, literal place is clear from the extensive physical and material descriptions given in Scripture. Ancient Jewish scholars also repeatedly made reference to a "preexistent heavenly counterpart to the earthly Jerusalem, a city God has founded and built already in heaven."[2]

The fact John sees the city "coming down out of heaven from God" (Revelation 21:2) indicates that it existed previously. Further, there is no contextual or scriptural indication that this city was suddenly created prior to its appearance here. In fact, just the opposite is true. Jesus, on the night before his crucifixion, told his disciples, "In My Father's house are many dwelling places." Then he promised, "I go to prepare a place for you" (John 14:2-3). This preparation is part of what Jesus has been doing for these past 20 centuries.

In the same conversation that Jesus told his men that he was returning to the Father, he prophesied that he would one day come to take them to the house he has prepared for them. I believe the "Father's house" he spoke of that night is the New Jerusalem.

The Specifics About the New Jerusalem

John is next carried by the Spirit (or *in* the spirit) to a high mountain (Revelation 21:10). From there, he will enjoy a unique vantage point—one he will need in order to view the gargantuan size of the New Jerusalem.

The city is described as "having the glory of God" (21:11), shining brilliantly like a diamond. And one of the more unusual aspects of the New Jerusalem is the shape of it. The city will be a massive cube that measures approximately 1,500 miles long, 1,500 miles wide, and 1,500 miles deep (21:15-17). All told, the city will measure roughly 2,250,000 square miles. The base of this city, if it were superimposed on the United States, would cover an area from the border of Canada to the Gulf of Mexico, and from Colorado to the Atlantic Ocean.[3] We would almost have to be in space to get an accurate perspective of how big this city is.

The New Jerusalem will be a perfectly cube-shaped city. The holy of holies in Solomon's Temple was also shaped like a cube (1 Kings 6:20), and the New Jerusalem's shape alludes to the fact that it now serves as God's eternal dwelling place.

The New Jerusalem's walls will be 72 yards—or 216 feet—thick (Revelation 21:17). And they will be made of transparent jasper.

The city will have 12 gates—3 along each side—with an angel posted at each one. The presence of the angels no doubt symbolizes the protection of the city, though none will be needed. Written on the gates will be "the names of the twelve tribes of the sons of Israel" (verse 12). There will also be 12 foundation stones inscribed with the names of the "twelve apostles of the Lamb" (verse 14). The 12 gates will each bear the name of an Israeli tribe, and the 12 foundation stones will each bear the name of an apostle. This represents that the Father's house will be home to both Jews and Gentiles.

The foundation stones of the walls will be "adorned with every kind of precious stone" (verse 19). And the gates themselves will each be made from "a single pearl" (verse 21) The streets will be "pure gold, like transparent glass" (verse 21). We know nothing of this type of gold here on earth. However, in God's city, all things will be new. The transparent elements of the city will allow the light of God's glory to pass through them.

Only those whose names are written in the Lamb's book of life will be allowed to enter this city (verse 27). This exclusive residency will not be based upon the residents' goodness or good works. Rather, their tickets to paradise were punched on the cross, where Jesus Christ purchased their salvation with his blood. It is on his merit alone that anyone will have access to this supernatural city.

The crystal-clear water of life will flow directly "from the throne of God and of the Lamb" (Revelation 22:1). On either side of this river will be the tree of life (verse 2), like the one that was in the garden of Eden. This tree will yield 12 kinds of fruit every month, and its leaves will be for "the healing of the nations" (verse 2). But why would we need leaves for healing? Won't we be free from pain and disease? The answer is yes.

We won't need healing of any kind because there will be no sickness or suffering in the New Jerusalem (21:4). The word translated "healing" is *therapeia*, from which we get our English word *therapeutic*. Many Bible commentators believe the fruit from the tree may simply be for our pleasure. But its leaves may serve a different purpose, perhaps somehow enhancing our enjoyment of the city. The mention of healing here doesn't presuppose the presence of pain or hurt, but rather, likely refers to some sort of "bonus blessing" that comes from applying these leaves.

The Perfections in the New Jerusalem

Finally, we will enjoy absolute perfection in the new Jerusalem:

1. Perfect *blessing*, as there will no longer be any curse from sin, and no sin nature (22:3).

2. Perfect *government*, as the "throne of God and of the Lamb will be in it" (22:3). God will reign supreme, and all will be well with our souls. Imagine that!

3. Perfect *activity*, as his "bond-servants will serve Him" (22:3). We typically think of service as a subservient activity, like waiting on tables or cleaning the house. But service to the King in the New Jerusalem will involve assisting God with various fulfilling adventures, tasks, and duties. We can't even conceive of the joyful, gratifying, delightful, entertaining, and wonderful things we will get to do for our Lord!

4. Perfect *communion*, as we will "see His face, and His name will be on their [our] foreheads" (22:4). That which is impossible now in our mortal bodies and unglorified state will become reality in that future day. We can't see God now, but we will then. The level of our knowledge of God will be immeasurable, and the depth of our love and experience with him will be remarkable.

5. Perfect *world*, as the lighting, temperature, and overall ecological environment of the New Jerusalem will be far more life-giving than any previous "best day" on earth. Our vision will be flawless and our lungs will be filled with heaven's life-giving atmosphere.

6. Perfect *reward*, as we will reign with him forever (22:5;
2 Timothy 2:12; Revelation 3:21; 20:4). Eden and our
co-regency with God will at long last be regained in
the New Jerusalem. As the apex of his creation and the
crown jewel of his salvation, we will be given authority
over various aspects of his eternal kingdom. What will it
be like to co-reign and rule with the creator and king of
the universe? We will find out!

A New World Coming!

On the new earth, we will serve God, see God, know God, love
God, enjoy God, and reign with God. This New Jerusalem will be
a beautiful city in a beautiful world, re-created for us by a beautiful Savior. Surrounded by gold and all that is good, together we will
reach unimaginable heights of worship poured out to God and wonderful friendships with one another.

What was lost in Eden will be restored in the new heavens and
the new earth. At this time, Scripture's story will come full circle, cli-
maxing in a place only God could create.

As we contemplate this is our eternal destiny, we realize that "the
sufferings of this present time are not worthy to be compared with
the glory that is to be revealed to us" (Romans 8:18).

Why, then, should we settle for less than the very best God has
to offer us? And why wait to reap the benefits of this coming paradise? Heaven's future realities can help us cope with today's difficulties.
Focusing on the future helps bring the present into proper perspective.

May you think often of your eternal home. Why? Because it's
real. It's guaranteed. And it's *yours*!

There really is a new world coming!

Chapter 13

THE OFFER OF A LIFETIME

The God Who *Calls*

Revelation 22:17

It would be an understatement to say that John has been on an emotional roller coaster ride throughout this Revelation vision. He has been in constant sensory overload since the first words of chapter 1. Now the vision is coming to an end, and Jesus has some final words for his beloved apostle.

It may come as a surprise that the conclusion of a book like Revelation—full of judgment, wrath, sin, and torment—would also be filled with amazing words of comfort and hope. But that too is the nature of our God. The angel we first read about in Revelation 1:1 begins his final message by telling the apostle that every word he has heard in this vision is "faithful and true" (22:6). And why? Because it comes from *him* who is faithful and true (3:14; 19:11). This means that the words of Revelation can be trusted. We can depend upon them to be absolute, divine truth about Jesus, the churches, heaven, the coming judgments, the antichrist, the millennial kingdom, and the new heavens and new earth. Revelation is no more symbolic or allegorical than the crucifixion and resurrection of Jesus were. Like the prophecies concerning Christ's first arrival on earth, this book contains truths that will also be fulfilled literally, exactly as written.

Jesus then makes a statement—one that is meant to resonate in our minds: "Behold, I am coming quickly" (22:7). In fact, so important is this prophecy that he repeats it two other times in this chapter as a way to embed this in our conscience (verses 12, 20).

In the first of these announcements, Jesus follows up by repeating the promise of a blessing that will come to anyone who "heeds the words of the prophecy of this book" (verse 7). This is the same blessing offered in Revelation 1:3, and it serves as a sobering reminder of the fact that Revelation is not meant to merely satisfy our curiosity about the future, but to change our hearts and bring us into a deeper relationship with God. By this point in Revelation, the seven churches would have already read the book or heard it be read. But now comes the hard part for both them and us: to internalize the truths that have been revealed, and to respond to Christ's reprovals in chapters 2–3.

As is John's custom, he wants his readers to know that he personally *heard* and *saw* the things he wrote about in the previous chapters (22:8). John was an eyewitness to the glorified Christ, his evaluation of the churches, and to the prophesied apocalyptic judgments. He also wants us to *believe* that the new heavens and new earth will be exactly as he described them.

Sensing the vision is coming to a close, the exiled disciple is once again overwhelmed by the sheer magnitude of the truths that have been entrusted to him. At a loss for words, and also momentarily losing his reasoning, he falls down to worship at the feet of the angel who showed him these things (verse 8). The angel immediately rebukes John, reminding him that he is a fellow servant of John and the prophets and "those who heed the words of this book" (verse 9). This angel's ministry of delivering the vision to John lives on today whenever anyone encounters the book of Revelation.

John is then told, "Do not seal up the words of the prophecy of this book" (verse 10). This is in contrast to what the prophet Daniel was told concerning his own end-times visions (Daniel 8:26; 12:4-10). Daniel's prophecies were meant to be preserved so that future generations (especially the generation that would witness the end times—Matthew 24:34) would have access to them. The clearest understanding of his prophecies concerning the last days will be understood during the "end of time; [when] many will go back and forth, and knowledge will increase" (Daniel 12:4).

Scholar Thomas Ice notes that the phrase "end of time" is "found five times in the Old Testament. All five uses are found in the book of Daniel (8:17; 11:35, 40; 12:4, 9)."[1]

The Hebrew phrase "go back and forth" is not a reference to modern travel, but rather, to a diligent searching through the book of Daniel. This verb is used many times in the Old Testament to portray diligent searching or movement (2 Chronicles 16:9; Jeremiah 5:1; 49:3; Amos 8:12; Zechariah 4:10). And "knowledge" in Daniel 12:4 has a definite article before it in the Hebrew text, meaning "*the* knowledge."

I take this to mean that the book of Daniel will enjoy a resurgence of interest in the last days, as those who are alive during the tribulation (perhaps primarily Jewish people) will search through the book in order to discern the events of their day and gain specific knowledge. Today, we understand the book of Daniel better than Daniel did. But those who live through the tribulation will understand those prophecies even better than we do because they will see the time of their fulfillment! They will see Daniel's prophecies played out before their very eyes.

In Revelation 22:10, John is told not to seal up the prophecy given to him. The reason for this is that "the time is *near*," or literally, "at hand" (verse 10). Colloquially, we might say, "It's right around the corner." In other words, it's on God's calendar.

Revelation's events are close, my, friend.

Very close.

God's RSVP

All this information now brings the reader and hearer of Revelation to an important intersection. A response is not simply requested, but rather, *required* by God. In Revelation 22:11, he effectively says, "Now is the time to pick a side. Choose your path. Set your course. A decision must be made."

Jesus then repeats his previous proclamation: "Behold, I am coming quickly." Then he adds, "And my reward is with Me, to render to every man according to what he has done" (verse 12). The first of these announcements promises a blessing, but here, Jesus pledges to bring a *reward*. He is not referring to the second-coming judgment seen in Revelation 19, but rather, to the judgment seat of Christ, which takes place immediately following the rapture (1 Corinthians 3:10-15; 4:1-5; 2 Corinthians 5:10).

Reminding us of his sovereign identity as "the Alpha and the Omega, the first and the last, the beginning and the end" (Revelation 22:13), Jesus highlights again the supreme blessings of receiving forgiveness through him, which include having the right to the tree of life and entrance into the New Jerusalem.

The contrasting curse for those who reject him is found "outside," where "the dogs and sorcerers and the sexually immoral and murderers and idolators, and everyone who loves and practices falsehood" will be (verse 15). "Dogs" was a Jewish term used to refer to the unsaved and false teachers (Philippians 3:2). Here, the Lord is simultaneously issuing an invitation *and* a final warning, highlighting the differences between life in heaven with him and eternal torment in hell apart from him.

Last, Christ identifies himself as "the root and the descendant of David, the bright and morning star" (Revelation 22:16). The "root" signifies him as the source of David's descendants (Israel), which sets him apart as God, while the "descendant" establishes the fact that he was also man—the unique and eternal God-man. Because he fulfills both of these roles, he is the perfect mediator between God and man, and he has earned the right to sit on heaven's throne (2 Timothy 2:8; Hebrews 12:2). As the legitimate heir to David's throne, he is able to extend the offer of salvation to those Jews and Gentiles who encounter this book.

On the heels of this gracious invite, the Spirit and the bride join in, making an appeal to people and saying, "Come" (Revelation 22:17). Anyone who hears and believes the truths of Revelation can also extend the invitation (verse 17). And anyone who is thirsty for what Revelation, heaven, and Jesus offer can come as well (John 4:13-14; 7:38-39). To those who respond, Christ promises a level of heart satisfaction unlike anything this world can provide. He quenches the thirst of the parched soul and lifts the weight from the burdened heart (Matthew 11:28-30). And the water he gives saturates our innermost being with divine, eternal refreshment. Best of all, it's free (Revelation 22:17).

All we need to do is come.

That's it.

God does not require anyone to "get their life together" before approaching him. That's because of what he actually *does* require, which is righteousness and perfection. Due to our fallen state, we are totally unable to elevate ourselves to God's standard of character and sinlessness. In contrast to how some in Christendom portray our intrinsic "worth," the Bible describes every one of us as being extremely *un*worthy. According to Scripture, before God, we are:

- unrighteous (Romans 3:10)
- unable to seek God (Romans 3:11)
- useless (Romans 3:12)
- unafraid of God (Romans 3:18)
- unable to ever be good enough (Romans 3:20)
- full of sin, falling short of God's righteous standard (Romans 3:23)
- condemned and deserving of God's punishment (John 3:18, 36; Romans 6:23)
- unable to "accept the things of the Spirit" (1 Corinthians 2:14)
- dead in sin (Ephesians 2:1)
- controlled by the world (Ephesians 2:2)
- a slave to our flesh (Ephesians 2:3)
- a child of wrath (Ephesians 2:3)
- hopeless (Ephesians 2:12)
- dominated by Satan's domain (Colossians 1:13)
- helpless to come to Jesus by ourselves (John 6:44, 65)

And yet, he commands us to come—not by our own will, but because the Father is actively drawing us to his Son (John 1:12-13; 3:5; Ephesians 2:4-7). Given our condition—that we are destined for eternal wrath—the invitation "Come" is an expression of immeasurable grace and mercy.

The prophet Isaiah put it this way:

> "Come now, and let us reason together,"
> says the Lord,
> "Though your sins are as scarlet,

they will be as white as snow;
though they are red like crimson,
they will be like wool" (Isaiah 1:18).

Jesus offers to do for us what we could never do for ourselves—to forgive us of all our sins, washing them away and declaring us to be perfectly whole and positionally righteous in his sight (2 Corinthians 5:21). There are no other requirements other than to "believe in the Lord Jesus, and you will be saved" (Acts 16:31). That's what "coming to Christ" means. The biblical word translated "believe" signifies being persuaded to the point of *depending* on something or someone. It is more than simply intellectually acknowledging a fact or agreeing to a truth. Rather, it involves choosing to place trust in an object. It's more like the desperate trust you have in a parachute to open for you. Or the way you put your faith in an airplane or a pilot to safely carry you to your destination. You don't "half trust" in the plane and try to help out by flapping your arms like a bird. Obviously, that's absurd. Instead, you put all your faith in the airplane to fly you.

The same is true with regard to your salvation. It's an all-or-nothing proposition. In this case it is extremely important, for your eternal destiny hinges on your decision.

How God Brings People to the Faith

No doubt, most who are reading these words are likely already converted. So you may be thinking of a friend or loved one who needs Jesus and the salvation he provides. With that in mind, what does it take to convince someone of their need for salvation?

God uses many means to bring people to faith:

- difficult or tragic circumstances
- apologetics
- being confronted with Scripture

- Bible prophecy
- emotional struggles
- sickness
- death of someone close to them

But in all these things, it is the Spirit's job to convict people of their sin, not ours (John 16:7-11). Our job is to love them enough to present the truth. And it is their responsibility before God to believe (John 3:16; Acts 17:30).

Now Is the Day

During the tribulation, as it wears on, it will become increasingly difficult for unbelievers to repent and turn to God (2 Thessalonians 2:10-12). That is why Paul wrote in 2 Corinthians 6:1-2, "Working together with Him, we also urge you not to receive the grace of God in vain—for He says, 'At the acceptable time I listened to you, and on the day of salvation I helped you.' Behold, now is 'the acceptable time,' behold, now is 'the day of salvation'" (see also Isaiah 49:8).

Translated, Paul was saying it's a much better idea to say yes to God's offer of salvation while the door of the ark is still open. And the good news is that, as of right now, it is.

The invitation to salvation and heaven is such a simple yet eternally profound proposition! And it's one that every person inhabiting the planet must consider.

Granted, some of Revelation's prophecies stretch the mind almost to the point of appearing unbelievable. However, the reader is confronted by the undeniable reality that the one who authored Scripture's final letter is the same one who rose from the dead. And his resurrection effectively "preauthorizes" the reliability of everything contained within the book.

A Final Warning

Even so, because Jesus knows all too well the human heart and the mind of sinful mortals, he adds a final warning. On the one hand is the skeptic who refuses to believe these apocalyptic visions could be anything more than the rantings of a deranged and deluded old religious fanatic. And on the other hand are those who are so eager to see these visions come to pass that they seemingly find prophetic fulfillment in every news headline.

However, a third category also exists—those who detract from or add to what John has written in the 22 chapters of Revelation. To them, the author of Scripture issues a stern caution:

> I testify to everyone who hears the words of the prophecy of this book: if anyone adds to them, God will add to him the plagues which are written in this book; and if anyone takes away from the words of the book of this prophecy, God will take away his part from the tree of life and from the holy city, which are written in this book (22:18-19).

Revelation represents the completion of Scripture's canon, meaning that, as of Revelation 22:21, God placed his pen down and wrote nothing further. Not even a word. Therefore, the Bible is complete. And nothing can be added to his written revelation.

In recent history, however, we have seen numerous authors publish books as if dictated from the Lord himself. And self-proclaimed prophets and prophetesses have "garnished" Revelation's prophecies with some prophecies of their own. Whether it's proclaiming the fulfillment of prophecy in the present, predicting the identity of the antichrist for the future, or discounting the teachings of the book itself, God says without stuttering, "Do not alter what I have written, or there will be severe consequences."

And just for the record, the Lord means what he says.

Knowing without a doubt that Jesus will release the seal, trumpet, and bowl judgments lets us know he will also make good on this promise to protect the integrity of his Word and punish all who meddle with the message.

And this isn't the first time God has given this warning (Deuteronomy 4:2; 12:32; Proverbs 30:6; Jeremiah 26:2). God is jealous concerning his Word because it is an expression of who he is. Therefore, to attack or detract from that revealed truth is to offend the Holy Spirit, who inspired every word of Scripture (2 Timothy 3:16-17; 2 Peter 1:21). So to be safe, we should never tamper with the sacred text by adding to it or detracting from it.

Put another way, we can never authoritatively preach or say that which Scripture does not say.

And when we come to those portions of the Bible that are difficult to interpret, unclear, mysterious, or hard to understand, we must humbly confess our limitations, allow God his secrets, and give ourselves time to grow in our understanding.

Come, Lord Jesus!

Jesus' ancient call to come, along with his own prophecy that he is "coming quickly," are both proclamations that are as clear and compelling as they were on the day when John first heard them. And without any further revelation from the angel, the apostle is so naturally filled with the anticipation of Christ's return that he can only reply, "Amen. Come, Lord Jesus" (Revelation 22:20).

This last book of Scripture is God's final word.

His grand finale.

Because of it, those of us who have been persuaded should extend the offer and invitation to others to come to this Jesus as well. And once they do, they too will love him and long for his coming.

John's closing words are truly a blessing to those who have journeyed through the vision described in his book. And he concludes with this: "The grace of the Lord Jesus be with all. Amen" (22:21).

After that, there is nothing else for him to say.

As it turns out, this final book of the Bible is much more than a sensational collection of prophecies and end-times wonders meant to blow our minds. What God really wanted to show us, above all else, was himself. He wants us to know that he is a God who...

reveals the future

is glorious

reproves his church

is sovereign over the universe

is worthy to be worshipped

is full of wrath and judgment

is gracious to sinners

is faithful to fulfill his promises

reigns over his kingdom

recompenses the guilty

will re-create the heavens and the earth

calls the world to salvation

His character and attributes are the strong thread woven throughout Revelation's pages. May those truths clothe you until the very day you retire to heaven or are raptured to glory!

NOTES

Seeing God in the Story of Earth's Final Days

1. A.W. Tozer, *Knowledge of the Holy* (San Francisco: Harper Collins, 1961), 1.

Chapter 2—The Unfamiliar Jesus

1. Having been miraculously delivered from Pharaoh's tyranny in Egypt, the Jews soon set up base camp at Mount Sinai while their leader, Moses, ascended the mountain for 40 days and nights, where he would receive the revelation of God's law. However, not content to wait on that revelation to be given to them, they became impatient and created their own version of this God who brought them up out of the land of Egypt (Exodus 32:4). Before the golden calf (a pagan representation of Yahweh) they worshipped, sacrificed, feasted, and participated in out-of-control sexual revelry (Exodus 32:5-6, 25). And for this sinful, idolatrous corruption, God desired to obliterate them and re-create a whole new nation through Moses (Exodus 32:9-10).

   But Moses intervened, and God relented (verse 14). Even so, the generation that "loved God but didn't do theology" suffered a horrible penalty. First, Moses melted the golden calf, ground it into powder, scattered the powder on the water, and made the people drink it (verse 20). Then the sons of Levi, as instructed by Moses, slaughtered about 3,000 men that day (32:28). That may sound like an overly harsh penalty for making a statue.

   Some might argue that the Israelites' worship was sincere since, after all, they had not yet received God's revelation of himself at Sinai. Moses was taking *forever* to come down from that mountain. But whatever good intentions the people might have had, they were summarily rejected by God.

   Sincere? That's doubtful. Sincerely wrong? Definitely.

   But even if the people were sincere, sincerity never validates a person's worship. Only truth about God does (John 4:4-24; 17:3).

   Most likely, these ancient wayward worshippers had incorporated religious rituals left over from their years of Egyptian slavery, where that pagan culture had influenced their minds and saturated their perceptions of divine beings. And just to make sure they understood how critically foundational their ideas about himself were, the Lord began his Ten Commandments with the following words: "I am the LORD your God, who brought you out of the land of Egypt, out of the house of slavery. You shall have no other gods before Me. You shall not make for yourself an idol, or any likeness of what is in heaven above or on the earth beneath or in the water under the earth. You shall not worship them or serve them; for I, the LORD your God, am a jealous God, visiting the iniquity of the fathers on the children, on the third and the fourth generations of those who hate Me, but showing lovingkindness to thousands, to those who love Me and keep My commandments" (Exodus 20:2-6).

   So to create a false representation of God (either actual, physical, or in our minds) demonstrates no real love for God. Likewise, we cannot invent versions of Jesus that fit our own understanding or interpretation of him. It has been said that no one can rise above their concept of God. In other words, the degree of our worship and love for God is directly proportionate to our understanding of who he is.

2. The trinitarian nature of God is a concept that has befuddled theologians and believers for centuries. Nevertheless, because it describes the very essence of who our God is, it therefore

becomes essential to attempt to grasp this foundational truth. Augustine allegedly said, "If you deny the Trinity, you'll lose your soul. If you try to explain the Trinity, you'll lose your mind."

Admittedly, our limited mental capacities cannot fully fathom the concept of the Trinity. But like standing at the ocean's edge, we can still believe it and appreciate it without being able to fully comprehend the depth or breadth of it.

Of course, the word *Trinity* itself is not found in the Bible. Much like *incarnation, great commission*, or *rapture, Trinity* is merely a term coined to help us better understand a truth that is found and taught in the Bible. Tertullian (born c. AD 155) is believed to be the first to help crystallize the concept of the Trinity for the church. Plainly stated, the Trinity portrays God as three separate and equal persons, yet existing in one indivisible essence.

Three persons. Fully God. One essence.

Unfortunately, there are no earthly illustrations that adequately communicate this unique and divine reality. Even so, some people still persist in trying to find apropos illustrations that somehow break the code and solve the mystery. For example, an egg has three parts—shell, white, and yoke—yet it is still essentially one egg. Water has a combined chemical composition yet exists in three forms: water, ice, and steam.

However, these and all other illustrations fall far short of accurately portraying the essence of the one true God. Remember that when the Lord revealed himself to Moses, and the barefoot shepherd asked, "What is his name? What shall I say to them?," God responded, "I AM WHO I AM…Thus you shall say to the sons of Israel, 'I AM has sent me to you'" (Exodus 3:13-14).

The Hebrew word for "I AM" is *Yahweh* and signifies God as a supreme, self-existent, and eternal being. In other words, he simply is and has always been. He had no beginning and he will have no end. This effectively relegates the question of "Who made God?" into the nonsense category. For if God, by definition, is eternal and self-existent, then such a question cannot even be asked regarding him. By virtue of the fact that he is a self-existent being, he would logically have had no beginning, thus fundamentally invalidating the question itself. In other words, an eternal God cannot have a beginning because he is eternal. A person cannot ask, "Who caused the uncaused Being?" The question is self-contradictory and illogical.

The concept of the Trinity is not a brain bender. It's a brain *breaker*. And the only appropriate response is belief, humility, and worship. Instead of trying to figure it out, we should instead fall on our faces in reverent worship.

3. Among those in Scripture who returned from the dead are the following:

    • The widow of Zerephath's son, by Elijah (1 Kings 17:17-24)

    • The Shunamite woman's son, by Elisha (2 Kings 4:18-37)

    • The man who was raised out of Elisha's grave after his dead body touched Elisha's bones (2 Kings 13:20-21)

    • The widow of Nain's son, by Jesus (Luke 7:11-17)—this was the first miracle of this kind by Christ

    • Jairus' daughter, by Jesus (Luke 8:40-56)

    • Lazarus, brother of Mary and Martha, brought back to life by Jesus (John 11), who proclaimed himself to be "the resurrection and the life" (verse 25)

    • Multiple saints in Jerusalem when Jesus himself was resurrected (Matthew 27:50-53)

- Eutychus, a young man who fell three stories to his death after dozing off during one of Paul's sermons—the apostle rushed over to him and brought him back from the dead (Acts 20:7-12)

4. Once, John is told *not* to write—Revelation 10:4.

5. Moses' encounter with God's presence left him with a "glory burn," or a face that shone—all because he had spoken with God (Exodus 34:29-35).

Chapter 3—Letters to the Churches Then and Now, Part 1

1. For further study, I recommend *Can We Still Believe in the Rapture?* by Ed Hindson and Mark Hitchcock (Eugene, OR: Harvest House, 2018).

2. The Latin phrase *damnatio memoriae* is more modern in origin, but it accurately describes the sentiments of ancient Romans against disliked leaders.

3. Aaron Earls, "Small Churches Continue Growing—but in Number, Not Size," Lifeway research, October 20, 2021, https://research.lifeway.com/2021/10/20/small-churches -continue-growing-but-in-number-not-size/.

4. *Voice of the Martyrs*, https://www.persecution.com/whoweserve/.

5. The crown of life is one of five special rewards New Testament believers may earn. Here are the five crowns:

   1. The imperishable crown (1 Corinthians 9:24-25), awarded to those who run their race with faithfulness.

   2. The crown of rejoicing (1 Thessalonians 2:19), awarded to all those who have suffered sorrow, death, and pain for the cause of Christ (Isaiah 25:8; 51:11; Revelation 7:17; 21:4). To some degree, all believers will enjoy this crown.

   3. The crown of righteousness (2 Timothy 4:7-8), awarded to those who "have fought the good fight...[and] kept the faith" and to "all who have loved His appearing" (a reference to the rapture).

   4. The crown of glory (1 Peter 5:4), awarded specifically to pastors who shepherd the flock of God voluntarily and not for financial gain, not being demanding or overly authoritative, but living as examples to the flock.

   5. The crown of life (Revelation 2:10), which will be awarded to all believers, for all believers go to heaven. But those who suffer for Jesus and who love him in spite of their sufferings may enjoy more honor from Christ with this crown.

Chapter 4—Letters to the Churches Then and Now, Part 2

1. This quote is found online, but its original source cannot be ascertained.

2. Some appeal to Exodus 32:33, where the Lord said to Moses, "Whoever has sinned against me, I will blot him out of My book." But the book mentioned here was a register of the physically living, not the book of life, which lists those who were chosen from before the foundation of the world (Revelation 13:8). Charles Ryrie said of the Moses reference that "to be blotted out meant to experience an untimely death." So Exodus 32:33 would refer to death, not condemnation (Psalm 69:28).

3. The Greek word *philadelphia* appears six times in the New Testament (Romans 12:10; 1 Thessalonians 4:9; Hebrews 13:1; 1 Peter 1:22; 2 Peter 1:7; Revelation 3:7).

Chapter 5—A Trip to the Throne Room

1. John MacArthur, *Revelation 1–11* (Chicago, IL: Moody, 1999), 147.

Chapter 6—The Lion, the Lamb, and the Little Book

1. In Ezekiel 2:9-10, we see a similar scroll of lamentations, mourning, and woe.

2. Jeffrey M. Jones, "U.S. Church Membership Falls Below Majority for First Time," *Gallup*, March 29, 2021, https://news.gallup.com/poll/341963/church-membership-falls-below -majority-first-time.aspx

3. Jo Yurcaba, "Percentage of LGBTQ adults in U.S. has doubled over past decade, Gallup finds," *NBC News*, February 17, 2022, https://www.nbcnews.com/nbc-out/out-news/ percentage-lgbtq-adults-us-doubled-decade-gallup-finds-rcna16556.

4. Typically we think of angels as singing at the birth of Christ, but the Bible says they spoke, not sang (Luke 2:13-14).

5. These words are widely attributed to Oswald Chambers, but the original source is unknown.

Chapter 7—Planet Earth in Peril

1. Scripture portrays at least five expressions of God's wrath toward mankind. They are as follows:

   1. *Everlasting/eternal wrath, or hell*—a literal place of constant, conscious torment (Revelation 14:9-11). All unbelievers are currently under the sentence of this impending wrath (John 3:16, 36; Romans 9:22; 1 Corinthians 16:22; Ephesians 2:3; 5:6).

   2. *End-times wrath*—the outpouring of God's judgment on planet Earth and its inhabitants during the coming tribulation period (Revelation 6–19). It is from this wrath that God promises to deliver Jesus' bride (1 Thessalonians 1:10; 5:9).

   3. *Catastrophic wrath*—this includes cataclysmic judgments on a nation or people, such as the global flood (Genesis 6–9) or the plagues upon Egypt (Exodus 7–11).

   4. *"Harvest" wrath*—wrath that God has ordained as a natural consequence to sin this side of eternity. What a person, people, or nation sows is what they will also reap (Galatians 6:7-10; see also Job 4:7-9; Proverbs 1:31-33; 5:21-23; 22:8; Hosea 8:1-14; 10:12-15). God says that if you plant sin in your life, it will produce a harvest of judgment. Theses consequences can happen naturally or as a direct judgment from God. Though the reaping is not always immediate, as a general rule, it does occur eventually. The principle of sowing and reaping also applies positively to good actions.

   5. *Abandonment wrath*—this judgment from God occurs when he releases a person or society, delivering them over to their own sin without any intervention or help from heaven (Romans 1:18-32). In the Old Testament, God's anger burned against Israel on many occasions, provoking his discipline. But we also see this abandonment wrath exercised against Israel as well, albeit temporarily (Psalm 81:12; Hosea 4:17; Acts 7:38-42). Because we are his children, God has promised to never abandon us (Matthew 28:18-20; John 6:37-39; 10:27-29; Romans 8:33-39; 2 Timothy 2:13; Hebrews 13:5). He has not, however, made this promise to Gentile nations. "Judgment preachers" attribute natural disasters to God, but divine abandonment is not about hurricanes, earthquakes, and natural disasters. Rather, it's about God *letting go*.

2. Romans 8:3; 2 Corinthians 5:21; 1 John 2:2.

3. Matthew 27:46.

4. Romans 6:23.

5. Genesis 6:5-6, 11-13; see also Matthew 24:37.

6. Compare with Matthew 24:7.

7. This word is also used to describe the color of grass and vegetation at the time of the first trumpet judgment in Revelation 8:7; 9:4; see also Exodus 9:18-26.

8. There are several views concerning these wild beasts. One view states that animals will become ferocious and deadly during the tribulation due to a thinning food supply brought on by war. The other view sees them as representing the antichrist and his kingdom leaders, who will destroy human life. The Greek word itself is explicitly used this latter way elsewhere in Revelation.

9. Matthew 24:7-8; Luke 21:11.

10. Matthew 24:9-10.

11. The martyred believers of Revelation 6 do not receive their glorified bodies until the end of the tribulation (Revelation 20:4). However, here, they do appear to possess some sort of temporary heavenly bodies, as they are wearing robes.

12. See Zechariah 14:6-7 and Acts 2:19-20.

13. Isaiah 26:4.

14. See Romans 1:18-21; 2:14-16.

15. How do we explain all the green grass being burned up in the first trumpet judgment, but green grass is later seen in Revelation 9:4? This is easily explained by the following:

    1. There is a time lapse between the first and fifth trumpet judgments (9:4). This allows time for grass to grow again.

    2. In most parts of the earth, grass isn't green all year around. So this speaks of the burning of all the green grass *at the time of this particular judgment.* This would leave the remaining grass untouched. Bottom line: All that is green at this time will be destroyed.

16. In the Old Testament, the word is associated with bitterness, poison, and death (Deuteronomy 29:18; Proverbs 5:4; Jerermiah 9:15; 23:15; Lamentations 3:15, 19; Amos 5:7; 6:12).

17. Isaiah, Ezekiel, Joel, Amos, and Jesus all predicted this phenomenon (Isaiah 13:9-10; Ezekiel 32:7-8; Joel 2:10, 31; 3:15; Amos 8:9; Mark 13:24; Luke 21:25).

18. This is the prison where some demons are kept by God (Luke 8:30-31; Revelation 11:7; 17:8). Satan is later cast into this abyss (Revelation 20:1-3).

19. We see the word "torment" (Greek *basanizo*) used elsewhere in Revelation (11:10; 14:11; 18:7, 10, 15).

20. Genesis 6:1-2; Jude 6-7.

21. In the New Testament, those tormented by demons lose control of themselves, suffering under the demon's rule over them (Mark 9:22). The similarity here is that even the ability to choose death is denied those who bear the mark of the antichrist.

22. The Bible never records that righteous angels are ever bound, as these four are.

23. Revelation 9:15.

24. Combine Revelation 6:8 with 9:15.

25. See Genesis 19:24, 28, where fire and brimstone are used in judgment.

26. These are all called plagues in verse 20. Other plagues mentioned in the remainder of Revelation include 11:6; 15:1, 6, 8; 16:9, 21; 18:4, 8; 21:9; 22:18.

27. Jeremiah 17:9; 2 Thessalonians 2:10-12.

28. Deuteronomy 32:17; Psalm 106:36-37; 1 Corinthians 10:20-21.

29. John 3:19-21.

30. Robert Thomas, *Revelation 8–22: An Exegetical Commentary* (Chicago, IL: Moody, 1995), 54.

31. See also Galatians 5:20; Revelation 18:23; 21:8; 22:15.

32. Genesis 6:1-2; 19:1ff. For more on how Noah's world parallels our own, See Jeff Kinley, *As It Was in the Days of Noah* (Eugene, OR: Harvest House Publishers, 2014/2022).

33. Margo Kaplan, "Pedophilia: A Disorder, Not a Crime," *New York Times*, October 5, 2014, www.nytimes.com/2014/10/06/opinion/pedophilia-a-disorder-not-a-crime.html?_r=0. See also John Rossomando, "Conference Aims to Normalize Pedophilia," *Daily Caller*, August 15, 2011, http://dailycaller.com/2011/08/15/conference-aims-to-normalize-pedophilia/.

34. Compare with Romans 1:18-32.

35. Revelation 16:10-11.

36. Hebrews 10:26-27.

37. The two "last trumpets" are distinguished in the following ways:

    • One occurs at the rapture, and the other at the midpoint of the tribulation.

    • One is for the benefit of the church, while the other has no significance to the church.

    • One happens in a moment/instantaneously, while the other over an extended period of time (the last half of the tribulation).

    • One is associated with rescue, while the other deals with wrath.

    • One concludes the church age, while the other concludes tribulation judgments.

    • One is the "last trumpet" in the church age while the other is the last trumpet of the tribulation period judgments.

    • No Scripture passage links the two "last trumpets" as being the same.

    • In 1 Corinthians 15:52, the trumpet is called "last" because of when it takes place (at the end of church age) rather than in relation to previous trumpets.

38. This is the same Greek word used in the Septuagint (a Greek translation of the Old Testament, or LXX) to describe the plague of boils in Exodus 9:9-11 and Job's boils in Job 2:7. It also is used in Luke 16:21 to describe the condition of Lazarus the beggar.

39. There is some evidence that suggests believers will be protected from this judgment (Revelation 7:16).

40. See Daniel 11:40-45, where the antichrist will receive troubling "rumors from the East and from the North" (verse 44). This is likely a reference to the kings of the East crossing the Euphrates and heading toward Israel.

Chapter 8—The Last Great Awakening

1. National Humanities Center, "Benjamin Franklin on Rev. George Whitefield 1739," PDF download, http://nationalhumanitiescenter.org/pds/becomingamer/ideas/text2/franklin whitefield.pdf.

2. Steve Pettit, "The Welsh Revival, *BJU Today*, February 16, 2018, https://today.bju.edu/president/the-welsh-revival/.

3. Dwight Pentecost, *Things to Come* (Grand Rapids, MI: Zondervan, 1958), 262-63.

4. In Ezekiel 9:1-11, God's prophet brings a message of his judgment to everyone in Jerusalem because of their apostasy. Only those who groan over the abominations of Jerusalem will be spared from the angelic "executioners of the city" (9:1). A cherub angel was to place a mark on the foreheads of the men "who sigh and groan over all the abominations which are being committed in its midst" (verse 4). Having God's mark meant you would be spared from his judgment. Interestingly, the word translated "mark" is *tav*, the last letter of the Hebrew alphabet. In ancient Hebrew script, *tav* was written like an x or a cross +.

5. Deuteronomy 17:6; 19:15; Matthew 18:16; John 8:17; 2 Corinthians 13:1; 1 Timothy 5:19; Hebrews 10:28.

6. Depending on how one interprets Revelation 13 and antichrist's return from the dead, this may be the only real resurrection between the rapture and Revelation 20.

7. Harriet Sherwood, "Israel earthquake could kill 7,000, disaster forecasts claim," *The Guardian*, Ocober 25, 2013, https://www.theguardian.com/world/2013/oct/25/israel-earthquake-kill-7000-disaster-forecasts-erden.

8. In Revelation 17:5, Babylon the great is the mother of prostitutes ("mystery Babylon," referring to the apostate world religion that permeates the planet at the beginning of the tribulation in preparation for the worship of the beast).

9. Julia H. Johnston, "Grace Greater Than Our Sin," https://hymnary.org/text/marvelous_grace_of_our_loving_lord.

Chapter 9—The King Finally Returns

1. "At doom's doorstep: It is 100 seconds to midnight," *Bulletin of the Atomic Scientists*, January 20, 2022, https://thebulletin.org/doomsday-clock/#nav_menu.

2. Eric Cline, *The Battles of Armageddon* (Ann Arbor, MI: University of Michigan Press, 2002), 142.

3. Some also include in this sequence the fall of Babylon (Isaiah 13:19; Jeremiah 50:9, 13-14, 23-25, 40, 43; 51:31-32).

    Studies in Earth's crust in this region have led Israeli seismologists to warn that a major quake is expected at any time. "The Christ Quake," *Evidence for God from Science*, November 10, 2013, https://discussions.godandscience.org/viewtopic.php?t=38866.

    Also, a fault line was discovered under the Seven Arches Hotel on the top of the Mount of Olives during the time of its construction. "Its presence prohibited the Intercontinental Hotel (now called the Seven Arches Hotel) from being built on the brow of the Mount of Olives overlooking Jerusalem as originally planned. It was re-located to the south and built on more stable ground where it stands today." Jason Keyser, "Jerusalem's Old City at risk in earthquake," *NBC News*, January 16, 2004, https://www.nbcnews.com/id/wbna3980139.

4. Ron Rhodes, *The End Times in Chronological Order* (Eugene, OR: Harvest House, 2012), 173.

5. The Jordan/Dead Sea Valley is part of a "continental transform"—a tectonic plate boundary between the Arabian and African plates. Running across this transform are geologic folds formed by when the two plates collide. Experts expect a major earthquake soon. *The Times of Israel* staff, "After tremors, experts warn a huge quake is the greatest threat facing Israel,"

The Times of Israel, July 14, 2018, https://www.timesofisrael.com/after-tremors-experts-warn
-a-huge-quake-is-the-greatest-threat-facing-israel/.

6. Hebrews 4:12.

7. 1 Timothy 4:6; 1 Peter 2:2; Hebrews 5:11-14.

8. Matthew 7:24-29; 16:15-18; Ephesians 5:25-26; 2 Timothy 3:16-17.

9. 2 Peter 1:3-4.

10. Compare Revelation 19:15 with 14:18-20 and Isaiah 63:2-3.

11. Revelation 14:20. Whether this is meant to be taken literally or not, it pictures the massive bloodbath Christ will evoke among untold millions who have gathered to fight him at Armageddon.

Chapter 10—The Lord's Prayer...Answered!

1. 1 Kings 4:21.

2. Jesus is at the right hand of the throne of God in heaven. But he is not yet reigning upon the Davidic throne of the millennial kingdom.

3. Dwight Pentecost, *Things to Come* (Grand Rapids, MI: Zondervan, 1958), 374.

4. John F. Walvoord, "Amillennialism from Augustine to Modern Times," Bible.org, https://bible.org/seriespage/4-amillianniallism-augustine-modern-times.

5. In Revelation 5:11, John uses another number, "myriads," which is the number 10,000 in Greek. But rather than communicate a specific number, in its context here, John is expressing a number that is beyond calculation and comprehension. That is why he multiplies it by itself. He is specifically being vague by using the plural form of this number, intending to communicate that the number of the angels and the redeemed were *innumerable*. In fact, in Luke 12:1 and Hebrews 12:22, the same word is used to express this numerically vague concept.

Chapter 11—The Court of No Appeals

1. Robert L. Thomas, *Revelation 8–22, An Exegetical Commentary* (Chicago, IL: Moody, 1995), 434.

2. Revelation 20:10, 15; 14:10; 19:20; 21:8; Matthew 3:10-12; 5:22; 7:19; 13:40, 42, 50; 18:8-9; 25:41; Mark 9:44; Luke 3:9, 16-17; John 15:6; Hebrews 10:27; Jude 7.

Chapter 12—There's a New World Coming

1. Ed Hindson, Mark Hitchcock, and Tim LaHaye, *The Harvest Handbook of Bible Prophecy* (Eugene, OR: Harvest House, 2020), 148.

2. Buist M. Fanning, *Exegetical Commentary on the New Testament* (Grand Rapids, MI: Zondervan, 2020), 531.

3. John MacArthur, *Revelation 12–22* (Chicago, IL: Moody, 2000), 282.

Chapter 13—The Offer of a Lifetime

1. Thomas D. Ice, "Running To and Fro," *Scholars Crossing*, Liberty University, May 2009, PDF download, https://digitalcommons.liberty.edu/cgi/viewcontent.cgi?article=1030&context=pretrib_arch.

OTHER GREAT BOOKS BY JEFF KINLEY

In *Aftershocks*, bestselling author Jeff Kinley reveals how current societal and global trends foreshadow the nearness of the end times—and how the prophecies about what is to come should renew your passion to lovingly proclaim Christ to a suffering world.

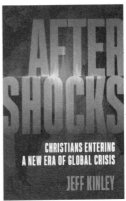

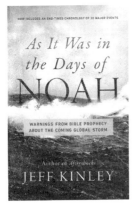

As It Was in the Days of Noah reveals the parallels between the time before the flood and our current culture, highlighting the rise in evil, the surge in immorality, and the pandemic of godlessness. This book equips believers to live wisely, making their days count for eternity.

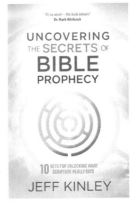

The future may seem like one big mystery—but it doesn't have to be! God has made his plans evident to all. And when you know what he has revealed, you can face the last days with a confident assurance of His provision and victory.

What happens when a country glories in its immorality, turning away from faith in God and obedience to him? This forthright survey of current events and trends offers valuable perspective on the future of America—along with powerful motivation to embrace the only source of lasting hope.

Jesus said, "Wake up and strengthen the things that remain." *Wake the Bride* was written to arouse a sleeping church to prepare for Christ's return. Many are unaware of the signs of the times. Others seem consumed by end-times hype. Jeff Kinley shows that our primary concern should not be the timing of Christ's return, but rather, the spirit and character he desires in his bride. Includes overviews of Jesus and his coming, the church and its mission, heaven and judgment, Satan and the antichrist, and other themes of Revelation.

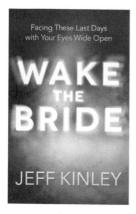

To learn more about our Harvest Prophecy resources, please visit:

www.HarvestProphecyHQ.com

HARVEST PROPHECY
An Imprint of Harvest House Publishers